Economic Controls and Defense

Economic Controls and Defense

By DONALD H. WALLACE

olmes
, 1903-

with a chapter on
Basic Problems and Policies
By J. M. CLARK

The Twentieth Century Fund
New York, 1953

MANUFACTURED IN THE UNITED STATES OF AMERICA
BY THE GALLERY PRESS, NEW YORK

Foreword

GOVERNMENT CONTROLS over the nation's economic activities are always a crucial problem when a major war is upon us—or seriously threatens us. Nothing could be further from the theory and practice of normal times than this sort of interference with our cherished freedoms. But experience has proved that controls are absolutely essential in times of extreme crisis and that the American people then accept and support them.

The leading questions, still unanswered, are: when is a crisis extreme enough to require controls, and what controls are called for? Recent history shows that the Korean war and the defense emergency were enough to cause a wide reimposition of controls—which had been abandoned as rapidly as possible after World War II. It also shows that the economy has since become productive enough to meet the demands both of defense and of increased living standards—and that strong fiscal measures and credit curbs, together with the growth in output, have enabled removal of direct price and wage controls without resumption of inflation.

The malaise of a major war threat has at this writing been diagnosed by the present Administration to be more chronic than immediately acute; but, like all chronic ailments, it is subject to a flare-up that would menace the civilized world. Apparently we may face a defense effort of fifteen to twenty years or more—an effort large by contrast to the peacetime past although far below the needs of all-out war. In a way this easing of tensions is a better time than crisis for a dispassionate study of economic controls—of when and how they should be used—to the end that we shall be better prepared to use them as occasion may require.

This is the fourth and final volume of a series of studies, begun in 1950, of how to protect and maintain an effective civilian economy while achieving the needed defense mobilization. Each one deals with the dangers that threaten our economic life in times like these and suggests constructive policies to guard against them.

The entire series has been produced under the direction of Albert Gailord Hart, Professor of Economics at Columbia University, with the active advice and counsel of a committee of four distinguished economists with special competence in this field: John Maurice Clark, *Chairman,* John Bates Clark Professor Emeritus of Political Economy, Columbia University; Theodore W. Schultz, Chairman of the Department of Economics, University of Chicago; Arthur Smithies, Chairman of the Department of Economics, Harvard University; and Donald H. Wallace, William Church Osborn Professor of Political Economy and Director of the Graduate Program, Woodrow Wilson School of Public and International Affairs, Princeton University.

This book, by Professor Wallace, treats the use of direct controls over materials, manpower, prices and wages. The first three chapters introduce the subject, explain the dangers to be expected from inflation and from undue use of direct controls, and pose the question how to minimize both evils. Chapter 4 develops rules of the game to tell when direct controls are needed and when they may safely be removed. Chapters 5-10 treat direct controls in use. Types and standards of control are examined from the dual standpoint of attainment of the objectives requiring their use and minimum interference with the basic values and institutions of a free society.

In Chapter 11, Professor Clark, Chairman of the Committee, analyzes the basic problems with which the report is concerned and sets forth the policies he believes are called for to meet them. In doing so he has attempted to express the consensus of the Committee, but minor dissents of other members are recorded in footnotes here and there.

The first report, entitled *Defense without Inflation,* written by Dr. Hart and published in April 1951, outlines the economic, political and military challenge of a long-sustained defense effort. It critically examines the major threats to the civilian economy—chief of which, of course, is inflation—and the various policies for dealing with them.

The second report, entitled *Financing Defense,* published in August 1951 and written by Dr. Hart and E. Cary Brown, concentrates on "budget measures" to finance the defense program and yet avoid a serious inflation—the various ways in which federal revenues might be increased to meet the necessary costs of mobilization without damage to the American economy.

The third volume in the series—*Defense and the Dollar*—written by Professor Hart, deals with the highly technical, but crucial, subject of the use of monetary and credit policies in the prevention and control of inflation.

With the publication of this fourth and last volume in the series the Fund expresses its deep appreciation to each of the authors and to the Committee which has worked so closely with them. They have rendered a genuine service to the public in these times of peril when calm analysis and wise counsel are at so great a premium.

EVANS CLARK, *Executive Director*
The Twentieth Century Fund

330 WEST 42D STREET
NEW YORK 36, N. Y.
JULY, 1953

Author's Preface

THIS BOOK deals principally with fundamental problems raised by use of direct controls in a long defense period—problems which we have never before had to face. There are no easy solutions to these problems. I do not claim to give complete or final answers. I have tried merely to set out the true issues, to chart the right direction for our thinking, and to stimulate further study and discussion. I have not attempted a detailed examination and appraisal of the direct control programs of 1950-1953. That would be another book.

I have benefited greatly from the help of others. John Maurice Clark, Albert G. Hart and Simon N. Whitney were patient enough to read the whole manuscript and give me detailed criticisms and suggestions. Gardner Ackley, Murray R. Benedict, Dean O. Bowman, Benjamin Caplan, David F. Cavers, Lester V. Chandler, Evans Clark, Robert L. Clark, John T. Dunlop, Richard A. Lester, Joseph E. McLean, Theodore W. Schultz, George A. Steiner and Paul J. Strayer have done the same for one or more chapters. Paul Trescott assembled facts and ideas for Chapters 5 and 6 and helped me with the analysis in those chapters. John Ladd did the same for Chapter 7. All those mentioned above have contributed to whatever merit this book may have. I have been unable to discover how to pin on them any of its shortcomings.

By skillfully performing the difficult task of translating academic jargon into ordinary English, Beulah Amidon has greatly improved the readability and clarity of every page. I am also indebted to Muriel F. Wilson for meeting so many peak loads cheerfully and converting so much incomprehensible scrawl into typescript with speed and efficiency.

I wish to thank Henry Holt and Company for permission to use here material originally published in somewhat different form in my chapters in *Economic Mobilization and Stabilization* by Lester V. Chandler and myself.

DONALD H. WALLACE

PRINCETON UNIVERSITY
JULY 1953

Contents

Tables

Economic Controls and Defense

1. Why Controls and What Controls

IN A DEFENSE PROGRAM, as well as in war, this nation must increase its economic effort and reorganize the use of manpower, facilities and materials, to turn out more munitions. This will inevitably mean inflationary pressures. Inflation hurts the efficiency of economic mobilization, robs people living on fixed dollar incomes and threatens democracy itself. To keep inflation within harmless limits means holding it down more than most people may realize.

We cannot increase and reorganize our economic effort and hold down inflation without more control over economic activity than we need in ordinary peacetime. An all-out war requires all-out control of the use of materials, facilities, manpower and credit, and of prices, wages, salaries, dividends and profits—in addition to very high taxes. Many of our peacetime freedoms must be suspended. But if the war lasts only a few years and is followed by genuine peace, these controls can soon be dropped.

Some Hazards of a Long Defense Program

If we face a period of ten, fifteen, twenty years or more in which 15 to 25 per cent of our national production goes to defense, we shall have to use, at least part of the time, government controls on prices, wages and profits, and on uses of materials, facilities and manpower. To avoid permanent injury to our basic values and democratic freedoms we must take care to limit these controls, in coverage and in time, to what is necessary for effective economic mobilization and the prevention of inflation. On the other hand, failure to control

3

inflation could mean permanent damage to American values and institutions.

Because the United States has a very rich economy we can use indefinitely 15 to 25 per cent of the total national production for defense—if we have to—without seriously affecting our standard of living. If we expand production rapidly we can soon produce more civilian goods each year than we did before the Korean conflict, in addition to a substantial output for the military. Average consumption per person can then resume its annual increase, although it may have to drop a bit at times to permit further jumps in defense production. However, defense need not at any time lower that part of consumption essential to health and general well-being. In 1952 total consumption of goods and services seems to have been about 3 per cent above the annual rate of the first half of 1950, although the total national output had risen by about 14 per cent.[1] With a growth in population of about 4 per cent this meant a very slight drop in per capita consumption.

The principal dangers in a long defense program are four:

(1) We may not devote a sufficient percentage of our resources to defense.

(2) We may accept chronic inflation, or successive doses of inflation, with serious political, social and economic consequences.

(3) We may permit government controls needed from time to time for economic mobilization and stabilization to harden into our institutions without realizing the issues involved.

1. See Council of Economic Advisers, *Annual Economic Review,* January 1953, p. 166.

(4) We may allow essential wartime controls to be discredited by overuse or misuse during the defense period.

The Readiness Program

The defense program, launched in 1950, calls for rapid build-up to a stage of "constant readiness" for war in both military and economic strength. One purpose is to raise the active personnel in the armed forces to 3.7 million and to train a reserve of several million more. Another is to build up stocks of planes, tanks, guns and other military equipment large enough for an initial brief period of full war, as well as for such limited military involvements as Korea. The goals set by the President in January 1952 are: an Air Force of 143 wings; an Army of 21 full-strength divisions; a Navy of over 400 active combatant ships and 16 large carrier air groups; and a Marine Corps of 3 divisions and 3 air wings.[2]

A third aim is the creation of reserve capacity for rapid expansion of military output to the levels needed in full war, should that occur. Provision of this reserve capacity consists of six things: (1) stockpiles of critical materials; (2) expansion of capacity of basic industries—materials, power, transportation, etc.; (3) large expansion of capacity for munitions production, so that plants used on a single-shift basis during the defense period can multiply output quickly by changing to round-the-clock operation; (4) spreading current defense contracts to ensure a wide base of firms with experience in war production; (5) increasing the ability to shift plants

2. *Sixth Quarterly Report of the Director of Defense Mobilization,* July 1, 1952, p. 8.

For more detailed description of the "readiness" defense program, see the first report in this series, *Defense without Inflation,* by Albert G. Hart, Twentieth Century Fund, New York, 1951, Chapter 3; and the other quarterly reports of the Director of Defense Mobilization.

from civilian to military production with a minimum of dislocation, temporary shutdown or migration of workers; (6) training additional workers in key skills.

Research and development of new, improved weapons are being pushed. Technical authorities say that the basic equipment of the fighting forces should be replaced every few years to avoid obsolescence and to maintain maximum fighting power.

The "readiness program" also includes military and economic aid to help other nations help themselves and us to prevent aggression.

Before the outbreak in Korea in June 1950 this country's defense budget amounted to about 7 per cent of the total annual production of goods and services. A year later, the defense program was taking about 10 per cent of national production. In 1952, the figure rose to 14 per cent. Already we have made considerable progress toward our goals. In mid-1952 it was intimated that the peak of the defense "take"—to be reached, perhaps, in 1953—would not exceed 18 per cent.[3]

At present, in February 1953, the new Administration has not yet said whether the scale of the defense effort can be reduced considerably, in a year or two, or will have to be further enlarged, even if there is no all-out war. The preponderant view seems to be that for an indefinite future the defense effort may have to be large, compared to defense spending in what we used to call peacetime. The problems treated in this book are based on the assumption that the de-

3. Council of Economic Advisers, *The Midyear 1952 Economic Review,* July 1952, p. 87. The total defense expenditure referred to here is the total of "national security" expenditures officially defined to include: military services, international security and foreign relations, development and control of atomic energy, promotion of merchant marine, promotion of defense production and economic stabilization, and civil defense.

fense take will average between 10 and 25 per cent of national production for many years to come. To us, these are new problems.

Why Controls Are Needed

Both maximum war effort and a defense program on the scale mentioned above involve the same basic problems, although differences in degree mean that there are some differences in needed control measures. Economic mobilization for war or for defense requires a country to devote a much larger proportion of its facilities, manpower and materials to three needs:

1. Maintenance of the active personnel of the Army, Navy, and Air Force;

2. Training of additional personnel for a military reserve;

3. Production of military equipment and supporting activities including military and economic aid to other nations.

From time to time there may also be a temporary heavy drain on resources for expansion of plant and equipment owing to the development of new weapons or change in the international situation.

Whether the proportion of the country's annual output of goods and services used for defense is between 10 and 25 per cent in a limited program or 50 to 60 per cent in total war, the goals of the program cannot be reached without a special set of government economic controls quite different from peacetime controls over economic activities.

The country cannot rely on voluntary enlistment to keep the active strength of the armed forces at 3.7 million, to say nothing of maintaining a trained reserve. Similarly, we cannot expect people and business voluntarily to cut spending for civilian goods to $40 or $50 billion less than they consider normal in relation to income, just because this amount is going to be spent by government on manpower, facilities and materials for defense production and supporting activities. Ordinary peacetime buying and selling practices and wage negotiations will not always ensure the flow of manpower and materials to defense plants in the needed amounts. Producers of civilian goods will naturally try to keep up output by retaining their labor and supplies of materials just as far as possible.

Holding Down Civilian Demand

Increased tax rates and stronger restrictions on credit, supplemented perhaps by wage and price controls, can reduce or hold down consumer and business demands. Priorities, allocations or other measures can assure to defense production the needed kinds and amounts of materials, facilities and manpower on time. Without such tax and credit measures and controls on materials, the government would have to bid these resources away from regular business and consumer uses by deficit spending. This would mean a continually expanding public debt.

It would also mean continuous inflation of prices and incomes because—in the absence of curbs on the regular spending of business and consumers—the added government spending would bid up prices and wage rates and raise total money income. And as the incomes of business and consumers rose, their ability to bid against the government would grow. To obtain the needed goods the government would have to keep raising its bids in an unending race to outstrip business and consumer demands. The resulting price rise would induce the hoarding of materials and manpower all along the line and encourage the growth of speculation and the multiplication of unnecessary middlemen. Inflation would also make impossible a general, no-strike agreement, which is imperative in wartime. Labor-management relations would deteriorate. Business planning and scheduling of production would be seriously hampered. The same would be true of government planning and scheduling of procurement. As living costs steadily rose, the morale of many persons, including those in the armed forces, would decline.

This is, in fact, not far from what happened here in the Civil War and even in World War I, when most economic controls were rudimentary.

Even under the best fiscal and credit measures, inflation may result from a surge of speculative or panic buying by business or consumers, financed by their existing liquid balances and savings, or from a spiral of price and wage increases. Direct price and wage controls may be needed to deal with such pressures.

During and since World War II we have learned much about the kinds of controls that can be effective in aiding economic mobilization and checking inflation. We can apply this knowledge to the problems of defense programs or all-out war; we can improve it by further study and experience.

What Is Meant by Controls

Controls to make possible effective mobilization of the country's economic resources and to prevent inflation include measures designed for any one of three purposes: (1) to influence the uses to which manpower, materials and facilities are put; (2) to limit the rate of spending by consumers, by business, or by local, state or national governments; (3) to keep levels of commodity prices and service charges, rents, and rates of wages, salaries, dividends and profits from rising above certain points.

In this book the word "control" is used broadly to mean any device or scheme designed for one of these purposes whether it is put into effect by a government agency, by one or more private groups, or by a board or committee made up of both public and private members. Thus the term "control" would include, in addition to government measures, an agreement by labor union leaders that wage demands should not exceed certain limits; a set of rules for rationing credit recommended to banks by a bankers' association or by the Board of Governors of the Federal Reserve System, or by both; rules to curb "labor pirating" recommended to firms in a given locality or region by a committee representing business, labor, and the federal and municipal governments.

In this book the term "government controls" will also cover much more than mandatory orders having the force of law with penalties for violation. The author includes requests by government to do or to refrain from doing certain things, and the establishment of incentives. An example of the first is a government request to all firms in an area of tight labor supply to hire only on referral from a central labor exchange. An example of the other is provision of better community services to attract more labor.

Direct and Indirect Controls

Controls are often divided into "direct" and "indirect."

Direct controls include two groups: (1) those that directly restrict the movement of specific prices or incomes—e.g., ceilings on prices, rents, wage and salary rates; (2) those that directly affect the use of specific materials, facilities or kinds of manpower, or place restrictions on production or consumption of particular things—e.g., priorities or allocations of materials, limitations on producing certain things, manpower priorities, and rationing of consumer goods.

Indirect controls are measures that indirectly affect prices, incomes and the uses of materials, facilities and manpower by limiting the total demand for everything or the demand in a broad field, such as real estate or consumer durable goods. When the income tax rate goes up people have less left to spend. An increase in personal income tax rates can lower total consumer demand below what it would be with the old rates. When a businessman has to pay higher taxes he may go slower in buying new plant and equipment. This kind of demand may also be restricted by curbs on bank loans. Total demand can be held down further by cuts in expenditures of federal, state and local governments.

When people buy homes or cars they usually borrow a substantial part of the purchase price and repay the loan over months or years. Hence the demand for new housing, for cars or for other large durable goods can be lowered by raising the size of down payments and rates of interest and by shortening the periods for repayment of loans.

When government uses *direct* economic controls (except pure incentive controls) the voluntary decisions of business, labor or consumers, and free competitive activity and free collective bargaining, are replaced to some degree by government regulation or by government influence. The extensive and prolonged use of direct controls would make great changes in our institutions. Within broad limits changes in tax rates, government expenditures, and terms of loan credit—the *indirect* controls—do not affect our institutions nearly so much.

Both direct and indirect controls are treated generally

in the first book in this series.[4] Indirect controls are the subject of two succeeding books.[5]

This book is about *direct* controls. It considers only briefly the problems of all-out war. Here attention is concentrated on the new, difficult problems of a long defense effort, which has to be much greater and more intense than in peacetime as we used to know it, but much less than in full war.

This is a book about basic issues of using direct controls. Its purpose is to reach discriminating conclusions with respect to the conditions under which direct controls are and are not needed, and the best principles and standards to apply when they are in effect. The book offers judgments on a few aspects of the direct control programs established in 1950 and 1951, but it presents no general or detailed evaluation of those programs or their effects. To make an informed and correct evaluation would require a whole study by itself.

All-Out Controls in All-Out War

Outbreak of another global war would require a rapid shift from the readiness economy to complete mobilization. The war effort would have to be very much greater than in World War II, partly because of the probable damage to life, industrial plants and cities at home, partly because the United States would have to carry a large share of the production and military effort from the outset, and partly because the enemy would presumably be geared to an all-out effort. Our survival would require much more extensive and

---

4. Albert G. Hart, *Defense without Inflation,* Twentieth Century Fund, New York, 1951.

5. Albert G. Hart and E. Cary Brown, *Financing Defense,* Twentieth Century Fund, New York, 1951.
Albert G. Hart, *Defense and the Dollar,* Twentieth Century Fund, New York, 1953.

drastic controls on the economy and on the population than those of World War II.

It would be necessary to devote to the war the largest feasible proportion of our national production—perhaps 50 to 60 per cent. Many consumer goods and services—automobiles, television sets, finer apparel and delivery services, for example—would have to disappear from the market or be severely restricted. Americans would have to get along with the bedrock, minimum standard of living necessary for health, morale and efficiency in the war effort.

The activation of the trained military reserve would take millions of men and women out of production into the armed forces. Fresh millions not normally employed would have to be drawn quickly into the labor force. Large numbers of people and large quantities of materials and facilities would have to shift into war production almost overnight. Conversion of civilian goods plants and their manpower would do part of the job. But a lot of people would have to move away from home to the locations of the big war plants. Extensive and effective controls over the uses of materials, facilities and manpower would be needed at the outset both to cut back civilian production and to get them into war uses in the right amounts at the right places. More steel would be required for guns and tanks. Its ordinary uses would have to be cut except where it was needed to expand war plants, to make railroad cars to transport war materials, or otherwise to further the war program. To permit mass production of planes, aluminum would have to be kept out of pots and pans, building construction and countless other uses, and large numbers of people would have to be drawn into the aircraft plants. And so on and on.

The immediate jump in government spending at the outbreak of war would be only the forerunner of an enormous increase in buying of war goods. If defense spending was running at about 15 per cent of the national product just before the war, it would have to climb, if possible, to three or four times that amount within a year.

Output of civilian goods and services would have to be cut drastically to make available all possible manpower, materials, plant and machines for war production. At the same time the public's income (before taxes) would increase as more and more individuals went to work and began to draw pay. It would rise still higher as weekly pay checks grew with an increase in working hours, and as many persons shifted to higher-paid war jobs.

Without all-out stabilization controls the amount spent by government, individuals and businesses—the total demand —would be very much larger than the supply of available goods at prewar prices. Hence inflation.

Taxes and Bond Sales

True, if taxes could be raised high enough (and soon enough) and if individuals and businesses also bought large enough amounts of war bonds, the total government receipts from both taxes and bond sales to the public could equal total government expenditure. In this case, individual and business income, after taxes and bond purchases, would not exceed the amount of the goods and services available at prewar prices. But in the face of the enormous cost of full war, taxes cannot be raised high enough, and people cannot be induced and probably cannot be forced to save enough, to achieve this balance.

In World War II, taxes amounted to only 40 per cent of the expenditures of the federal government, even with the sharp boost in tax rates. Sales of war bonds to individuals and businesses raised this by another 32 per cent.[6] In other words, only 72 per cent of government spending was covered by taxes and bond purchases by persons and businesses. The government had to borrow the additional 28 per cent from the banks. In four years, the banks handed over to the government for war spending $84 billion of new money in the form of deposit credits. Hence, the amount of money that individuals, businesses and government had to spend during the war was much more than enough to buy all available goods and services at existing prices. If we had not had price ceilings the prices of most things would have skyrocketed.

In another war, we should raise taxes somewhat higher than in World War II and sell more war bonds. But if taxes or forced bond buying were pushed too far, workers and businessmen might slacken their efforts to increase production. An all-out war program ought to take 50 to 60 per cent of the national production—much more than the 45 per cent in World War II. Revenues from taxes and bond sales would have to be almost three times what they were in 1952 to pay for an all-out war. It would probably be neither desirable nor possible to raise taxes and bond sales high enough to wipe out the "inflationary gap"—the gap between total demand and the total value of the available supply of goods and services at existing prices.

Hence ceilings on prices, wages, salaries, rents and dividends would be necessary to curb the self-propelling spiral of living costs, wages and farm prices. And extensive ration-

6. These figures cover the four-year period July 1, 1941–June 30, 1945. They are computed from data in Lester V. Chandler, *Inflation in the United States, 1940-1948,* Harper, New York, 1951, pp. 65, 67 and 72. For the fiscal year 1945 the figures were, respectively, 56 per cent and 32 per cent.

ing of consumer goods would be needed to help ceiling price control and controls on production and use of materials. In full war, the question is not whether inflation can be stopped without use of direct controls but whether inflation can be checked even with the greatest practicable use of all controls, direct and indirect.[7]

Controls in the Defense Period

The dangers to our values and institutions inherent in a prolonged defense effort are less evident and more insidious than those of an all-out war lasting only two, three or four years. With the grave emergency of full war and the resulting unity of purpose in the nation, inflation control is likely to be successful, at least during actual hostilities. If there is postwar inflation, as in 1919-1920, or 1946-1948, it is likely to be a quick, one-shot affair rather than a prolonged barrage—unless the "peace" is actually cold war, an armament race and sporadic outbreaks of limited fighting; in other words, the situation we now face. In such a situation we may be in increasingly serious trouble, unless we use all our knowledge to curb inflation whenever it threatens.

In a defense effort taking not more than 25 per cent of national production, fiscal and credit controls to hold down

7. It is, indeed, possible to design models for an anti-inflation control system without direct ceilings on prices and income rates that would prevent inflation if they could be made to work. Ingenious systems of this sort have been devised. They sometimes contain inconsistencies. Beyond this, confidence in such a system is based on the assumption that the scheme and all its parts would function at a point near perfection, an assumption out of accord with reality. It is much more probable that political difficulties would block legislation authorizing use of all parts of the system and that administrative difficulties would diminish further the actual accomplishments. If we really want to prevent inflation in full war we must use all known measures that can command political support and be administered effectively. This is not a neat way to do the job, but it is probably the only practicable way. Attempts to devise systems that would dispense with direct stabilization controls may, of course, lead to improved kinds of indirect controls.

demand for nondefense goods and services should be the primary, continuing defense against inflation, as emphasized in all the books in this series. "Pay-as-we-go" taxes ought to be the rule. Deficit financing should not be used unless it is the only practicable way to meet unavoidable, short peaks in defense spending.

Some hold that we can keep down living costs by ceilings on prices and wage rates alone, thereby avoiding higher taxes. They support their case by pointing to the effectiveness of price and wage ceilings in World War II in the face of enormous deficit financing. But they forget that the postwar inflation was due largely to failure to hold down *incomes* of individuals and businesses during the war to anything like the extent *prices* were held down. As a result the enormous accumulation of savings pushed up prices when they were spent after the war. All through the war, personal and business incomes were much larger than could be spent. Each year saw huge savings, much of them in government bonds, cash balances or other liquid forms. Before the war, individuals as a group had saved, on the average, 4 to 5 per cent of their annual income, except in the worst depression years. In the three war years 1942-1944 they saved 22 to 24 per cent of their income. After the war, individuals and businesses began to spend their wartime savings. This was a major reason for the sharp postwar inflation, which carried wholesale prices up 50 per cent from the summer of 1946 to the summer of 1948, and raised consumer prices by 31 per cent in the same period.

The Road to Inflation

In a defense period of indefinite length, to pay a large part of the cost of defense year after year by deficit financing would be a shortsighted, unworkable "have-your-cake-and-eat-it-too" policy. In fact, it would guarantee inflation, whether or not price and wage ceilings were in effect. For a few years most of us might save unusually large amounts to buy defense bonds. To be sure, these yearly amounts of "extra" savings would be relatively less than in World War II. But as the years went by the total would grow steadily. Sooner or later more and more men and women would want to work less or spend more of their savings—or both. If they spent any large part of their savings prices would be forced up immediately, unless ceilings were in effect. But even ceilings could not stem the tide for long. As savings piled up, more and more of them would go to market—the "black market"—and compliance with ceilings would break down. Presently confidence in the stabilization program, in the value of the dollar and in government credit would be undermined. Then would come virulent inflation, the worst kind, fed by fear that breeds fear as it goes along. With five, ten or fifteen years or more of large defense spending, this country cannot avoid serious inflation unless it follows the rule of budget balance or pay-as-we-go almost all the time.

Taxes, Credit Curbs and Direct Controls

In a defense program varying between 10 per cent and 25 per cent of national production, taxes can probably cover expenditures without being high enough to discourage productive efforts of business and labor. Whether such taxes are politically possible remains to be seen. The same must be said of restrictions on credit for nondefense purposes. But almost all economists agree that in a limited defense program fiscal and credit controls should be the primary, continuing defense against inflation.

Given effective indirect controls, can we do without direct controls in such a defense effort? Direct controls are essential in all-out mobilization, but that does not prove them necessary in a limited defense program. On the other hand, we cannot say that because they are not needed in "ordinary peacetime" they will not be needed in a defense program. The question cannot be answered "Yes" or "No," but only "It all depends." It is the job of Chapter 4 to supply the best available answer to this question. But it will point up the discussion in the next two chapters if we state here two of the major conclusions of Chapter 4.

1. Indirect fiscal and credit controls can limit total demand enough to free large amounts of resources for defense production, but they cannot deal with bottlenecks at particular points. A bottleneck is an acute shortage of a material—steel, aluminum, cotton linters or glycerin—or of a type of equipment or of manpower. Only direct controls can deal effectively with such scarcities. Many bottlenecks are to be expected in the early stages of a defense program. They will also occur when there are marked changes in the production program calling for large and sudden alterations in the relative volume of output of different munitions items—for example, more planes and fewer tanks, requiring more aluminum and copper and less steel.

2. Fiscal and credit controls cannot under all conditions do well the job of halting a spiral of interacting price and wage increases, or preventing a sudden surge of spending liquid savings. Direct controls will at times be necessary to deal with these problems, if we want to prevent inflation or at least keep it within tolerable limits. The question is: Which is more harmful—a certain amount of inflation or a certain amount of direct control?

Both chronic inflation and chronic use of direct controls would bring serious dangers to free, democratic institutions. These are described in the next two chapters.

2. The Dangers of Inflation

THIS COUNTRY'S MAIN JOB in the uneasy years ahead is to strive to ensure peace without aggression. This calls for many measures beyond the scope of this book, such as strengthening the United Nations, extending the Voice of America and other media of international communication, helping underdeveloped regions to "get started," changing our diplomacy as the world situation changes, strengthening democracy at home and continuously demonstrating to the world that we are working for peace.

A necessary part of our job seems to be a large defense program, including military and economic aid to other free nations. This may have to go on for a long time. If so, we face two kinds of danger.

On the one hand, inflation could destroy confidence in the dollar, rob people living on fixed dollar incomes, and threaten our democracy itself not only by promoting group strife but also by curtailing social services, religious activities and education. On the other hand, prolonged use of direct controls could slow up economic progress, limit flexibility in meeting consumer demands, and also threaten democracy by encouraging pressure groups to become more powerful and more belligerent or by producing an intolerable political stalemate.

These dangers may not be obvious. Let us see exactly what they are and how serious they might become.

Walking, Loping, or Runaway Inflation?

What sort of inflation do we have to guard against? The answer depends largely on how much we spend for defense. The danger from mounting defense spending may be no more than creeping inflation of 1 to 4 per cent a year, or it may be walking inflation of 5 to 10 per cent a year.

We do not know what will happen once this present readiness program is completed. If the defense take should go back to "ordinary" peacetime levels—less than 10 per cent—and stay there, this book could be thrown away. It might seem pleasant to worry once again about peacetime problems of inflation and depression.

If, on the other hand, defense requirements should rise steadily year after year, demanding a larger and larger part of national output, sooner or later this would carry us beyond a limited defense program. At some point—30, 35 or 40 per cent—the defense take would become so large that we should have to have a managed economy similar in kind, if not in degree, to that needed in full war. There would then be danger of galloping inflation, and full use of direct controls would be the least of various evils. In this situation, the problem would be to preserve democratic institutions in a managed economy. We shall not try to treat that problem between these covers.

This book deals mainly with the problems of a limited defense program that would not usually require more than 25 per cent or less than 10 per cent of our annual production. After we complete the build-up called for by the present readiness program the defense take may level out on a plateau of 12 to 15 per cent of national production and stay there for many years. In this case, the danger would be chronic inflation at a creeping (1 to 4 per cent a year) or a walking gait (5 to 10 per cent a year). The same would be true of a gradual, upward drift in the defense take carrying it, say, from 12 to 20 per cent in ten years—a "rising plateau."

Humps, Troughs or a Plateau of Spending?

However, the needed level of defense activities may not remain steady for a decade after the completion of the present build-up. From time to time there may be other such outbreaks as Korea, requiring military operations and the increase in personnel and equipment that goes with them. At times, changes in the international temperature may bring a rapid build-up for a few years. New weapons may alter strategic plans and demand a sudden increase in the output of particular types of military goods or, at least, of plant, equipment and manpower to produce them when needed. An extensive plant dispersal program, if it were to be carried through rapidly, would require the diversion of large amounts of manpower and equipment from other uses for a few years.

Should some of these things occur, there could be a succession of humps and troughs in defense spending. During the humps the potential inflation might be a loping 10 to 15 per cent a year, possibly more. Between the humps the fall in defense spending would probably lessen general inflationary pressure; there might even be some decline in prices.[1]

A plateau of defense spending would probably be easier to handle than humps. Fiscal and credit policies, once adjusted to the plateau level of defense expenditure, would need to be changed—as in ordinary peacetime—only to deal with changes in private or nondefense governmental activities that would alter the weight of the potential inflationary pressure. Most government controls on use of materials, facilities and manpower, most price ceilings, and government

---

1. It will be evident from the preceding three paragraphs that some of the problems posed in this book relate to a longer period ahead than those treated in *Defense without Inflation,* by Albert G. Hart.

wage controls could be removed after a few years as output caught up with demand nearly everywhere—if fiscal and credit policies were kept sufficiently strong, if the people came to expect stability, rather than inflation, and if there was reason to expect noninflationary private price and wage policies.

A succession of two- and three-year humps in defense spending would present a harder problem. Strong forces making for a spiral of price and wage increases, a surge of speculative or panic buying, and deficit financing—all these three causes of inflation are more likely to be active with a short, sharp hump than with a plateau. A buying spree and a spiral of prices and wages can begin quickly, as they did in the weeks following the outbreak of hostilities in Korea in June 1950. To prevent surges of inflation in the humps quick application of anti-inflation measures is necessary.[2] Unless this can be done, either at the discretion of the President or in accordance with some automatic formula, we would probably have periodic doses of inflation in the humps.

Our Bulwarks against Runaway Inflation

With a defense effort that takes no more than 25 per cent of the national production we need not fear a runaway inflation such as Germany suffered after World War I, or Hungary after World War II, when prices went up many thousand times, money became worthless, and savings in the form of money, insurance or bonds were literally wiped out. Our basic strength in economic resources, know-how and initiative, unimpaired by any substantial debts to other nations, is a bulwark against the inflationary pressure of a limited defense program. Also, the progressive income tax and the

2. This is spelled out in Chapter 4.

corporate profits tax would put strong brakes on galloping inflation. As money incomes of individuals and businesses rose, taxes would take larger and larger proportions of those incomes. Hence both individuals and businesses would have less and less of their larger incomes to spend. Moreover, we as a people know enough about the catastrophic effects of runaway inflation to be sure we want to avoid that tragedy.

Chronic inflation is the economic enemy in this defense period. With either the plateau or the humps we could have inflation most of the time for ten, fifteen or twenty years, averaging 4 or 5 per cent a year—perhaps much more.

Some say that, rather than inflation, we are likely to have declining prices much of the time for years to come. They point to the very heavy consumer spending in the years 1946-1950 to stock up on everything except perishables—including housing—and also to the very large business spending since World War II on plant expansion and modernization. They think this reflected large pent-up demands, resulting from the long period (in the Great Depression and the war) of abnormally low buying of housing, consumer durables, and business plant and equipment. When demand for all these things goes back to "normal," they say, even the defense spending will not offset the drop and prices will fall.[3]

Perhaps this is right. Only the event will tell. But it would be foolish to count on this theory and lay no plans to control inflation, which many consider more likely than deflation. If it turns out that we are not often bothered by serious inflationary pressure these plans can gather dust.

3. This view that deflationary forces will be dominant for many years, it must be made clear, is different from the view that there will be some deflation for a year or two after defense spending reaches its top in 1953 and levels off or drops somewhat.

Chronic Inflation

We Americans never have lived in a world where the outlook was chronic inflation for an indefinite period ahead at a rate averaging not less than 4 or 5 per cent a year, and perhaps more, with years of price stability or dips offset by surges of inflation. True, prices and living costs have jumped in wartime, but everybody expected the inflation would stop with peace and it did.[4] We have had some sharp price rises in booms followed by drops in depressions. The longest peacetime period of chronic inflation in the United States since the Civil War was the first ten years of the present century when the level of wholesale prices rose about a third, or an average of about 3 per cent a year.[5]

Between June 1950, when the Korean conflict began, and March 1951 the average of wholesale prices in the United States increased about 16 per cent and the average of consumer prices rose 8.4 per cent.[6] In the next twenty-one months (to December 1952) wholesale prices drifted down by about 6 per cent while consumer prices crept up by about 3.5 per cent. The general flattening out of prices in the spring of 1951 came chiefly from higher taxes, stronger credit restrictions, operation of price and wage controls and

4. From the latter part of 1948 to mid-1950 it looked as though the inflation of World War II and the 1940s had come to an end. But the growing realization that we were in an unprecedented situation, a "cold war," kept us on the brink of renewed inflation, which suddenly became a reality with the outbreak of fighting in Korea in June 1950.

5. The price rise from the low point of the depression of the middle 1890s —1896—to the cyclical peak of 1910 was about 50 per cent. But a good part of that rise was just normal recovery of prices from their depression low of 1896. To get a picture of chronic, noncyclical inflation it is better to compare 1899, a recovery year, with 1909 or 1910, which gives us increases of 30 and 35 per cent respectively.

6. Price figures are from the indexes of wholesale prices and consumer prices computed by the Bureau of Labor Statistics, U.S. Department of Labor.

allocations of short materials, the growth of inventories and the disappearance of scare buying.

Wage rates also increased in many fields during the two and a half years following the Korean outbreak. Indicative are the increases in average hourly earnings of about 21 per cent in durable-goods manufacturing, about 15 per cent in non-durable-goods manufacturing, about 20 per cent in building construction and about 13 per cent in retail trade.[7]

At the beginning of 1953 the indexes of consumer prices and wholesale prices stood about 12 per cent and 9 per cent respectively above their June 1950 levels. There were no signs of early renewal of general inflationary pressure. However, inflationary pressure may return in 1953 or 1954 if the international situation worsens, or if the scale of the defense program is stepped up for one reason or another, or if expectations of cuts in defense spending do not materialize. Let us suppose that in mid-1955 both price indexes were 16 per cent above their June 1950 levels. This would mean increases from their December 1952 levels of 3.5 per cent for the consumer index and about 6 per cent for the wholesale index.

Let us further suppose that most people began to think that at least this rate of price increase—an average of 3 per cent a year in those five years—was going to continue unchecked for ten, fifteen or twenty years. Chronic inflation, even at this creeping rate, could have grave consequences.

Inflation Destroys Confidence in the Dollar

With chronic inflation, people could not count on a stable

7. Increases in average hourly earnings may reflect shifts to higher-paying jobs, merit increases, "upgrading" of individual employees, more overtime hours worked and other factors, as well as increases in basic rates. In durable- and non-durable-goods manufacturing there were small increases in hours worked per week in these two and a half years.

dollar. They would have to expect a continuous (though not steady) fall in what a dollar would buy.

TABLE 1

HOW RISING PRICES AFFECT THE BUYING POWER
OF THE DOLLAR

| | Increase in Average of Consumer Prices at Annual Rate of: | | | | | |
| | 3 Per Cent | | 5 Per Cent | | 7 Per Cent | |
Period	Total Percentage Increase in Prices	Buying Power of One Dollar	Total Percentage Increase in Prices	Buying Power of One Dollar	Total Percentage Increase in Prices	Buying Power of One Dollar
End of 5 years...	16	$.86	28	$.78	40	$.71
End of 10 years..	34	.75	63	.61	97	.51
End of 15 years..	56	.64	108	.48	176	.36
End of 20 years..	81	.55	165	.38	287	.26

Note: The percentage increase in prices over each of the various periods is computed like compound interest. For example, a 5 per cent annual increase means that in the second year the increase is 5 per cent of 105 per cent, or 5.25; in the third year the increase is 5 per cent of 110.25 per cent, and so on. All figures in the table are rounded off to two places.

With a price rise of only 3 per cent a year, for example, the dollar would lose a quarter of its value in ten years and a third of its value in fifteen years. At the end of twenty years it would buy only 55 cents worth of what it bought at the beginning. With a yearly price increase of 7 per cent it would take only ten years to cut the value of the dollar in half. At 5 per cent a year this would occur in fifteen years. (See Table 1.)

The Real Value of Savings Impaired

Democracy emphasizes the worth of the individual and his freedom to use his abilities in the most rewarding legitimate opportunity he can find. A corollary of this freedom is the obligation to provide as well as he can for his dependents. In our system, he does this by saving dollars and putting them into various kinds of securities, retirement pensions or annuities (social security and private plans), savings accounts and the like. So invested, his savings are supposed to be secure. But in a long period of chronic inflation they would lose much, or most, of their value.

But what other investment is available? Many common stocks would increase in value with inflation, but some would not. And even in a defense period with general inflationary pressure most of the time, many stocks will fluctuate in value, in a way unpredictable to most investors. Many experienced stock market operators lose out even when it looks as though everything ought to go up. To buy stocks is no sure way for an individual to protect the buying power of his savings, even if he can spend all his time studying the market!

Real estate—building lots, houses, stores, etc.—ought to be a good investment in an inflationary period, and many real estate "parcels," as they are called, will prove so; but some will not. Many towns that produce ordinary peacetime goods would not have a real boom in a defense inflation. In these, real estate values would not rise in step with inflation in the country at large—or with living costs at home. And even in boom towns some pieces of real estate would not be good investments. For those who can afford it, purchase of a home can indeed protect people against some part of the inflation in housing costs, but this represents only a part of their living costs.

To buy real estate or stocks is no sure or safe way to guard the real value of savings of those in the middle- and lower-income groups in a period of chronic inflation. In fact, in such a period individuals would have no sure way to protect

the real buying power of their savings without the development of some special means to this end.

A long period of chronic inflation that destroyed the value
of billions of dollars of savings might result in less and
less saving—"only a sucker will save when the value of the
dollar is going down and down." There would probably be
a growing number of persons who had no confidence in the
dollar and were bitter because their savings were melting
away or because they could see no safe way to provide for
their future.

Fear of a steady drop in the value of the dollar would
make it hard to manage the large debt of the federal government. As notes and bonds come due, the Treasury, unless
it has a surplus, usually sells new ones to provide funds to
pay off the old. A surplus is not usual. With the value of the
dollar falling steadily could the Treasury sell to individuals
and businesses enough new securities from year to year to
pay off the old ones, except at very high interest rates—which
would jump the yearly cost of carrying the debt—or with
the promise that interest payments and redemption payments
would go up automatically in dollars whenever the price
level rose? Of course, if the Treasury had to sell the new
securities to banks, this would increase the money supply and
feed the inflation.

Effects of Inflation on Contracts

But more than savings and government finance are involved here. At stake, also, are the integrity and workability
of the whole system of financial contracts for payment for
services, for work of all sorts, and for goods. The efficiency
of our economic system and the economic freedom of individuals and groups are promoted by the institution of finan-

cial contracts between persons or organizations governing terms of employment, sale of goods, and loans—contracts extending over days, weeks, months, or years, and all expressed in dollars.

With chronic inflation and growing distrust in the value of the dollar such contracts would increasingly become unworkable. Transactions would go more and more on a "spot" basis; or contracts would have to provide that the amount of the payment would automatically be adjusted upward by the amount of inflation during the life of the contract. The escalator clauses increasingly brought into wage contracts in the postwar inflationary years are a familiar example. Under these, wage rates are automatically raised or lowered at stated intervals in step with the movement of the consumers' price index of the Bureau of Labor Statistics.

Chronic inflation would destroy public confidence in all dollar contracts and thus tend to discourage initiative and savings, unless the contracts provided for escalation of dollar payments in step with inflation. This does not seem a likely development, at least for some years to come.

Chronic inflation averaging a few per cent a year will not produce economic collapse and paralysis as will runaway inflation. But in the long run the gradual undermining of our financial contract system might be even more deadly to enterprise and to economic freedom.

People Living on Fixed Incomes Suffer

Inflation of prices hurts everyone whose income does not increase in step with the rise of prices. The worst injury is suffered by older people dependent on inflexible modest incomes that do not increase at all—the so-called "fixed" incomes from annuities, pensions, savings bonds, and the like.

During the war the average of the prices of consumer goods and services in this country went up about one third. In the middle of 1946, it took about $1.33 to buy what $1.00 bought in 1940. To put it another way, the real purchasing power of a dollar had dropped to $0.75. A widow with an annuity of $200 a month found that this would buy only what she could formerly get for $150.

The postwar inflation of 1946-1948 and the upsurge of prices after the Korean outbreak have carried the average of consumer prices to about 90 per cent above the level of 1940. (See Table 2.) The $200 annuity will now buy only as much as $104 would purchase in 1940. Its value has been cut almost in half.

TABLE 2

THE CONSUMERS' PRICE INDEX AND DOLLAR VALUES,
1940-1952

Year	Consumers' Price Index	Value of the Dollar
	(1935-1939 = 100)	
1940 Monthly average	100.2	$1.00
1946 June	133.3	.75
1948 Monthly average	171.9	.58
1949 Monthly average	170.2	.59
1950 Monthly average	171.9	.58
1950 June	170.2	.59
1951 Monthly average	185.6	.54
1952 November	191.1	.52

Source: Bureau of Labor Statistics. The consumers' price index measures changes in the prices of consumer goods and services bought by moderate-income families in large cities.

A person who bought a $75 savings bond right after Pearl Harbor and received $100 for it ten years later—his original investment of $75 plus $25 interest—found that his $100 could buy in December 1951 no more than $58 would buy when he purchased the bond.[8] In effect, he not only drew no interest; his original investment of $75 had lost nearly a quarter of its value.

Older people dependent on fixed incomes are becoming a steadily larger part of our population. Chronic inflation would pinch them severely in their declining years unless an increasing part of their support were taken over by their children, other relatives or charities, or their "fixed" incomes were raised to make up for the rise in living costs. The possibilities of such adjustment would probably depend chiefly on the source of the income, whether it came from federal old-age and survivors' insurance, from pension plans of business, government agencies or other institutions, or from individual savings in the form of bank accounts, bonds, insurance policies or annuities.

In a long period of chronic inflation Congress would probably escalate federal social security payments, but there might be quite a lag in this. At any given time, Mr. Jones might find that his payment had been raised only enough to cover two thirds, or three fourths, of the advance in living costs.

Many business corporations might increase benefits under their private pension plans. But even so, would payments keep step with the price inflation? The prospect of timely and adequate escalation is even less in the case of retirement benefits of state and local governments. Local governments depend largely on revenues from the property tax and these seldom keep pace with inflation. Tax systems of many states do not yield increases geared to price inflation. The tax sys-

---

8. In December 1941 the consumers' price index was 110.5. In December 1951 it was 189.1. These figures are from the "old" index for which the average of prices in 1935-1939 equals 100.

tems of many local and state governments would have to be altered markedly to yield such increases in revenues.

Those dependent on income from their own savings accounts, bonds, insurance policies or annuities individually purchased would have no prospect of periodic increases in income from these, unless or until banks, governments and other bond issuers, and insurance companies guaranteed to raise payments and redemption values as prices rose; or Congress decided that all such incomes should be raised regularly as living costs advanced, presumably with the federal government carrying a part of the financial burden.

Guarantee by the federal government would probably be the only sure way to give full protection against inflation to beneficiaries of pension schemes of private business enterprises and state and local governments. Perhaps it would be better both for individuals and society if most people stayed at work beyond present conventional retirement ages. But surely there are less costly ways of accomplishing this than by inflation.

Inflation Harms Those Whose Incomes Lag

What about those who live on wages and salaries? Will all wage and salary rates keep up with the inflation of living costs? Obviously not. Revenues of local governments and many state governments lag behind inflation; they cannot raise the pay of all their employees to keep up with inflation. Policemen, firemen, teachers, doctors, dentists, nurses, accountants, highway workers and other employees of state and local governments—some or all of these will be hurt by inflation. The same is true of many employees of private educational, philanthropic and religious institutions. Employees of some public utilities will also have difficulty in getting wage advances to keep up with living costs because the utilities can obtain rate increases only after months or years of hearings or litigation. The wages and salaries of employees in many branches of private business, also, will tend to lag, at least from time to time, behind the inflation of living costs. Inflation never hits evenly.

The foregoing is not to say that individuals, groups, businesses and governments would never find ways of so adjusting the conduct of their affairs as to obtain partial or sometimes even complete compensation for inflation. Indeed, the longer chronic inflation lasted the greater would be the endeavors to that end. Insurance companies, savings banks and companies operating private pension schemes would invest less of their funds in bonds and mortgages and more in "equities," such as stocks and real estate. Individuals could do the same, buying shares in investment trusts to spread the risk. But equities involve some risks even in chronic inflation, so it is doubtful whether all savings would go over into equities. Instead, there would probably be increasing demand for securities on which interest and principal would be paid in dollars of constant purchasing power.

Perhaps some day all contracts extending over more than a quarter or a half year will provide payment in terms of dollars of constant purchasing power, according to an appropriate price index—contracts between sellers and buyers of goods and services, employment contracts, bonds, bank loans and other loan contracts, insurance, annuities, pensions and so on. Difficult problems would be encountered in working out such arrangements; the federal government might have to underwrite such "purchasing power" guarantees in all private contracts, including pension plans, if they were to be "sure fire." Many private organizations cannot be sufficiently sure of their incomes to *guarantee* payments that keep up with inflation. Universal use (or anything like universal use) of contracts in dollars of constant buying power seems a long way off.

The Damage to Education

Only a well-educated people can have the understanding, the tolerance and the self-discipline required to make democracy work in the increasingly complex modern world. Chronic inflation would impair the quantity and quality of education in many public and private schools, colleges and universities because teachers' salaries in many instances would lag behind the rise in living costs or salary increases in competing occupations.

The *average* salary of a public school teacher was raised enough in the late 1940s to offset the inflation of living costs accompanying World War II and its aftermath. But many teachers did not receive increases sufficient to match the rise in living costs. Between 1938 and 1950, the average salary increase for public school teachers in cities of 50,000 population and over was reported as a little over 70 per cent.[9] This was about the same as the average increase in consumer prices in cities as shown by the consumers' price index of the Bureau of Labor Statistics. But the average increase for teachers in cities of 500,000 population and over was only 56 per cent; and the average increase for teachers in the whole group of cities of 50,000 population and over was only 47 per cent in Middle Atlantic states and 63 per cent in Mountain states.[10]

9. Bureau of Labor Statistics, *Wage Movements, City Public School Teachers,* Series 3, No. 5, Supplement No. 1, p. 1.

10. *Ibid.,* p. 2. In the period 1939-1949, the average increase in teachers' salaries in cities of 50,000 and over was 62 per cent, yet 2 out of 5 of these

The statistics also indicate that in the decade 1940-1950 salary increases of superintendents, principals and other administrative officers in the public schools were in general proportionately less than salary increases received by the teachers.[11]

It is common knowledge that even where teachers' salaries kept ahead of the advance in living costs, they often lagged behind pay increases in other fields. The current teacher shortage reflects these facts. Some teachers have resorted to part-time work in other occupations to supplement their academic salaries. This usually means that they give less time to preparation for classroom teaching, to furthering their own education, or to participation in such important extra-curricular school activities as discussion clubs, music, debating and dramatics.

In colleges and universities, even the average of teachers' salary increases has failed to keep up with the inflation of living costs beginning with World War II. Here most teachers have suffered a reduction in real income. State institutions as well as private colleges and universities suffer financial stringency in inflation.[12]

---

teachers received increases of less than 50 per cent, and one out of 5 had raises of less than 35 per cent. In cities of 500,000 and over, about 7 out of 10 teachers got increases of less than 50 per cent, and 4 out of 10 received increases of less than 35 per cent. See Bureau of Labor Statistics, *Wage Movements, City Public School Teachers: Salary Trends, 1925-1949*, Series 3, No. 5, April 1951, pp. 6 and 7.

11. National Education Association, *Research Bulletin*, Vol. XXIX, No. 2, April 1951.

12. *The Impact of Inflation upon Higher Education*, an interim statement by the Commission on Financing Higher Education; and H. K. Allen (in collaboration with Richard G. Axt), *State Public Finance and State Institutions of Higher Education in the United States* (a staff study for the Commission on Financing Higher Education), Columbia University Press, New York, 1952.

The Squeeze on Individuals, Institutions and Communities

This may give us a preview of what would happen in a prolonged period of inflation. Many cities and towns would find it difficult to maintain teachers' salary increases geared to inflation unless state governments or the federal government came to their aid. Many state colleges and universities also would be pinched. The financial squeeze on state and local governments would result in curtailment of building and equipment plans as well as of teaching force. The result —continued use of old-fashioned buildings and equipment, overcrowding and overlarge classes.

Privately endowed universities and colleges would be severely squeezed. Perhaps they could raise tuition in step with inflation, but this would not be enough. A substantial part of their revenue comes from returns on endowment, much of which is invested in bonds or other low-risk securities with fixed or semifixed incomes. Also, they are heavily dependent on annual gifts from alumni and others merely to cover running expenses, to say nothing of new buildings and equipment. It is uncertain whether or not annual giving can keep step with inflation.

Education has been one of the foundations of American democracy. Chronic inflation would undermine education. At first, the deterioration would not be obvious. When teachers refuse to engage in extracurricular activities outside school hours unless they receive extra pay, and the extra pay is not forthcoming, the deterioration is evident. But John and Mary are not likely to report any change in the teaching of arithmetic after Mr. Smith starts to drive a taxi at night. Caesar's *Commentaries* may not seem any more baffling to high school sophomores after Mrs. Brown begins to work evenings in the public library. And the boys and girls in the civics class may not realize that the forceful and facile Mr. Hope, who is adding to his salary by writing speeches for a pressure group leader, has become, consciously or unconsciously, an advocate of a special interest in class discussions.

It might also be a long time before the citizens began to realize that when teachers have a growing feeling of bitterness and frustration, and a hardening conviction that the only way to obtain fair treatment is by power tactics, they cannot be the best teachers of tolerance, cooperation, equality of opportunity, compromise and other basic elements of democracy.

Effects on Religion and Social Services

One can scarcely doubt that chronic inflation would bring somewhat similar results in religious activities. If the clergy and their associates are more dedicated than lay teachers, they are still human beings. With costs rising faster than revenues, endowed religious institutions would suffer the same squeeze as would private educational institutions.

Privately endowed social services would have the same experience. Inflation would tend to curtail the activities of endowed hospitals, the YMCA and YWCA, the Red Cross, settlement houses, boys' and girls' clubs, and kindred activities and agencies.

Social services provided by city, town or other local governments would suffer in the same ways and for the same reasons as the public schools. Here, also, the federal government doubtless would take over some of the load sooner or later, directly or through grants-in-aid, but probably not on a scale to permit normal increases in quality and quantity— perhaps not even enough to maintain existing levels.

The conclusion that increased federal aid probably would

not be sufficient to prevent impairment of social services and education rests partly on experience. It is also supported by the consideration that in a long period of inflation Congress and the Executive would be under increasing pressure to economize, to keep down taxes and to combat inflation. Educators and social workers do not seem to have as much political power in Washington as many other groups. And although the "consumers" of education and social services are legion, most of them have no concerted political power.

Social services are a bulwark of democracy. Aid to the handicapped and disadvantaged, a helping hand to those who need a fresh start, medical care for those who need it, provision of recreational facilities, organized athletics and hobbies and out-of-school programs for millions of children —these are stars in our democracy that should shine more brightly for all the world to see, instead of suffering a dim-out because of inflation.

Inflation Breeds Strife among Groups

Inflation is bound to increase group strife.[13] Perhaps a large majority of businessmen, farmers and employees of private business would be able to keep up with the rising living costs over the years. But from year to year some would be behind, some ahead. Few, if any, groups would dare count on automatic protection without efforts of their own. Chronic inflation would put a premium on group organization to consolidate power and on fighting tactics. Thus it would intensify existing rivalries and hostilities among groups—between labor, management, and farm groups, and among various farm, labor and business groups themselves.

A principal element of democracy is freedom to hold, to

13. Cf. Hart, *Defense without Inflation,* pp. 15-17.

express and to act on differences in values, opinions and judgments. Democracy thrives on such differences, but not on the attitudes and tactics of warfare. In a prolonged inflation, group after group would gird itself for the struggle to protect its interests—or to advance them at the expense of others in order to provide a reserve against possible future defeats. Internal strife in our society is already serious. How long democracy could survive with increasing internal tension nobody knows. To find out by experiment would be a game of Russian roulette.

In these troublous times, our democracy is under great strain from pressures within and without. Inflation would increase this. If we seriously want to preserve democracy— as, of course, virtually all Americans do—we will take no chances with chronic inflation.

3. The Dangers of Direct Controls

PROLONGED USE OF DIRECT CONTROLS in the defense period would bring dangers as serious as those of chronic inflation. The controls might "wear out" and hence be impaired in value if they were needed in full war. On the other hand, they might harden into our system and lead to a managed economy whether or not the country really wanted that. Long use of direct controls might also result in an increase in group power and a struggle threatening the existence of democracy. At present, February 1953, the new Administration is rapidly removing most of the direct controls established in 1950 and 1951. They may be needed again from time to time during a long defense period, so we should ponder the dangers of unduly long use.

Controls May Wear Out

Direct controls, if long used, might so deteriorate that they would not be much good in all-out war, when we would need them badly and need them in first-class working order.[1] Over a period of several years, there could be a lot of "wear out," as more and more persons became sick and tired of the restrictions and the annoyances of regulation and as more ways and more ingenious ways were discovered to "beat the game." Nothing so discredits a control system as failure to work effectively and equitably. Moreover, as we saw in Chapter 1, price and wage controls would break down sooner or later, given continuous, large increase in the money supply

1. See Hart, *Defense without Inflation,* pp. 96-97.

42

and money incomes of individuals and businesses and a resultant piling up of abnormally large savings.

Should war break out when direct controls were in general disrepute, it might be difficult to re-establish quickly general acceptance of stringent direct controls, yet without them maximum economic mobilization would be impossible. "Keep your powder dry" has always been a good watchword in time of trouble.

Controls May Harden into Our Institutions

After several years of direct controls dislike of them may always become so widespread that Congress will remove them —whether or not they are still needed. And there will be times during the defense period in which we do not need direct controls to prevent inflation—provided fiscal and credit measures are sufficiently strong.

Direct controls may not always kill themselves off, however, and indirect controls may not be made strong enough and kept strong enough to prevent inflation. There probably will be political opposition to removal of price control at almost any given time, unless most prices have actually fallen below ceilings and the public is confident that they will not go up again soon. When prices were at ceilings, the public would expect them to rise after decontrol, and many prices probably would. If the choice seems to be between higher taxes *or* price control, price ceilings may often seem to be a better bargain—even when they really are not—because the impossibility of holding down inflation year after year in the face of inadequate fiscal policy is not understood.

Moreover, it can often be argued that a new inflationary threat may be "just around the corner." In an uneasy international situation a new flare-up, leading to a new defense build-up, may occur at almost any time. For this reason, many will say it is unwise to scrap price, wage and allocation controls and dismantle the control agencies.

We seem to come to this: Perhaps direct controls will always be removed after a few years, because so many get sick of them, or because they are no longer needed and a sufficient majority realizes this. But there is also a real possibility that direct controls will sometimes be kept for many years —whether needed or not—because many fear that inflation will follow decontrol, or because a new inflationary crisis seems to be imminent in this world of international tension.

Prolonged use of direct controls would raise serious questions of change in some of our basic institutions—in free collective bargaining, freedom of individual businesses to set their prices, freedom of producers to introduce new products. Wage control—if it is genuine—necessarily sets limits to the results of collective bargaining. Also, price ceilings necessarily restrict the freedom of businesses to set their selling prices. With materials under allocation by government order, the freedom to develop new products may be restricted. Government regulation, or at least government influence, in the form of direct controls, replaces to some degree individual or group decisions, free competitive activity and free collective bargaining. This is not true where incentives alone are used, as, for example, in shifting manpower into defense plants or in converting plants to war production. But apart from the field of manpower, where mandatory regulation may not prove effective even in war, the twin jobs of organizing defense production and preventing inflation involve both direct controls of a restrictive sort and those using incentives.

Of course it is true that in a democracy the effectiveness of controls on prices, wages, jobs and products depends primarily on widespread acceptance and compliance, rather than on policing. "Chiselers" have to be policed, but the controls will fail of their objectives unless nearly all comply voluntarily. However, this does not alter the fact that these controls curtail the economic freedom of the individuals and groups who comply, as well as the freedom of those who have to be policed. And there will always be some to urge that spreading noncompliance must be met by more "crackdowns" and more power for enforcement authorities. Up to a point these may be necessary, but somewhere along this line democracy is endangered.

Influence of Public Opinion

After relatively short, intense emergencies like those of the two recent world wars, it is not difficult to lay aside most of the temporary direct controls. But if in a defense period we use direct controls for five or ten years, they may harden into our institutional setup, and stay there.

The great majority of Americans in all major groups do not now want to replace the free decisions of individuals and groups, free competitive activity and free collective bargaining with a large extension of central government direction of economic activity. Of course, we as a people will want, and will make, many future changes in our institutions, as we have in the past. The one unchanging rule about human institutions is that sooner or later they always change. But we Americans want, so far as possible, to decide what changes we are going to make in our institutions by established democratic political processes, free from the hasty compulsions of emergency situations. We do not want to "back into" basic changes.

Perhaps the longer direct controls are kept in effect the

more likely they are to be junked in the end. But if a growing number come to feel dependent on direct controls, the controls may become permanent even though more effective indirect controls would actually make them unnecessary.

To the timid, and to some of the prudent, the familiar things usually seem preferable to the unknown—so perhaps the longer we have the direct controls, the more people will favor keeping them. Or perhaps controls popular with politically powerful groups may be kept and others abandoned even though this results in unfairness. Moreover, decontrol may never seem politically feasible if labor groups strongly oppose removal of price control, and farm groups strongly oppose removal of wage control and limitations on corporate profits—even though no group with political power actually wants all these controls kept.

If direct controls should harden into our institutions over ten, fifteen or twenty years it would probably be necessary to extend government authority in other fields as well as in these. If for many years we should have central government control of most prices, wages, profits and use of resources, the present "mixed" system of free enterprise and free collective bargaining plus considerable government regulation or influence would be well on the way to transformation into socialism—a system under which government makes the principal decisions as to what is produced, the relative amount of investment and consumption, and prices, wages, salaries and profits. There are degrees and variations of socialism. For a time, it need not involve the nationalization of many industries, although this might be the ultimate outcome if the motivations of capitalistic enterprise died out.

The American people do not want to make decisions about fundamental changes in institutions by a series of disconnected choices, scattered through emergency years in a crisis climate. To avoid this we must take the long view, be certain that we are clear on the issues, and find guideposts to be sure we know at each turning point what we are doing.

Government Management Instead of Free Bargaining

Direct government controls mean that in large measure Congress and government agencies rather than bargaining in free markets determine prices, wages and profit rates, what to produce and how much of each product.

Our market system is not perfect. Many markets are not highly competitive. Some are too competitive—or would be, if they were left to themselves. Other faults have been pointed out by students of the system. By and large, however, the markets do respond to changes in consumer demand.

If people want more beefsteaks and roasts, as compared with other kinds of meat (as they have in recent years), the prices of choice beef cuts and of steers go up. The margin between the price of beef animals and the price of feed widens. Farmers and cattle raisers breed more cows and feed more animals for slaughter. Within a year or so, the supply of steaks and roasts in the stores has expanded and beef prices are coming down again (unless all prices have gone up in a general inflation in the meantime).

When the ladies want nylon rather than rayon stockings, the "market" quickly transmits this news to producers of nylons in the form of increased orders from retail stores and wholesalers. If nylon hosiery makers have already set their prices to yield a good profit margin the prices may not be raised. But if their profit rates have been low, or if their larger demand for nylon (the material) results in a rise in its price, they may increase their prices for stockings.

The Influence of Consumer Demand

If those who are eating more beef buy less pork, pork prices will fall and hog production will be discouraged. As consumers shift to electric refrigerators, fewer old-fashioned iceboxes are sold. Orders for them from retailers and wholesalers drop; producers cut output and to stay in business they may have to cut prices.

Thus the market mechanism telegraphs changes in consumer demand to manufacturers, producers of raw materials, farmers, importers and others. Sooner or later producers respond by increasing the output of the things more in demand and reducing the output of things of diminishing appeal. Increases or decreases in orders all along the line are the main sign of changes in demand. Price increases or decreases are also important signals in markets where prices change quickly and often sharply—such as farm products, cotton textiles, lumber and scrap metals. And in all kinds of markets, changes in prices and profit rates may be necessary in some cases to induce the desired increases and decreases in output.

Wage rates tend to be higher, or to go up faster, in industries with growing sales than in those where sales are steady or falling. This helps steer manpower to the places where it is most needed.

Now it would not be *impossible* for a central government agency to do all this by direct controls so that changes in consumer demand would be matched roughly by the desired changes in output of the almost innumerable products, and appropriate changes in prices, wages and profit rates would be made.

This would require a complicated accounting system and an enormous staff to keep track of changes in consumer spending on the various products and other pertinent indicators. Some imperfections would obviously exist. The facts would not always be clear to officials. A minimum of honest mistakes would be unavoidable. The number of would-be "fixers" would probably grow and there might be an increase in corruption. Moreover, some officials would be tempted to gear production to give the public "what people ought to have" rather than what they wanted. There would always be the danger that those with command of political votes could influence government decisions more effectively than consumers with economic votes, expressed merely in the way they spent their dollars. And it would be difficult for public control to afford as much flexibility in prices, qualities, styles and the like as we have in free markets.

The imperfections of direct control in meeting changes in consumer demand might be much greater than those of the present system of free market bargaining. In any case, this market system, with its more or less automatic response to shifts in consumer demand, is a much more economical way. Government control would involve great numbers of government employees. Staffs of pressure groups would be enlarged to bring maximum pressure on government officials with tons of statistics and the lengthy documents that lawyers call "briefs." (More about pressure groups in the next section.)

Toward the Goal—Increased Productivity

A good economic system will not only meet shifts in consumer demand, but also show steadily increasing productivity. Rising productivity in most of the economy is the only way to raise real incomes and living standards for all of us. This is especially true in a period when a considerable part of total output has to go to defense. Increased productivity comes chiefly from advances in technology and administration. Both management and labor can contribute substantially to this.

Would prolonged use of direct controls speed or slow up increased productivity? The answer is not clear. In general, inflation discourages advances in productivity by diverting the efforts of management and labor into quicker and more direct means of keeping up with inflation—getting price and wage increases, building up inventories, and the like. In a period of strong inflationary pressures, direct controls that help stifle inflation may thus contribute to raising the national productivity to levels that otherwise would not be reached.

On the other hand, application of direct controls for several years might slow up advances in productivity as a result of squeezes on profits or wages, here and there; inability to get the materials needed for improved processes; or simply because of uncertainty about future rules on prices, wages and availability of materials. Advances in productivity that come from new firms might suffer most—because government finds it hardest of all to make rules for new firms. With direct controls in effect, managements almost surely will spend more time, effort and money on trying to influence government decisions, and this may mean a lower rate of increase in productivity than would occur if they devoted more attention to production.

On balance, the direct control system might do a poorer job than the free-bargaining market system both in meeting shifts in consumer demand and in advancing productivity. Thus it would not seem sensible to scrap our present system, unless we are sure we want a different system and are prepared not only to operate it but at the same time to keep a healthy, vigorous political, economic and social democracy.

This is particularly important if, as suggested earlier in this chapter, the hardening of direct controls into our system over the years would extend greatly the central government management of economic activities and their results. We do not know whether or not it is really possible to have central government direction of the economic system and at the same time retain political democracy and a large measure of personal freedom. This is a grave question; as yet, it is unanswered. In the uneasy years ahead, our democracy will be under severe strain. It seems wise to go slow on institutional changes that raise tough problems as to the maintenance of political democracy and personal freedoms—when solutions are by no means clear.

Pressure Group Struggles

Whenever legislatures or executive agencies of government take the responsibility of controlling economic activities, interest groups have an inducement to become as powerful as possible, and to use pressure tactics. When the market decides things, it is hard to find anybody to blame for results you do not like. When government decides, it is easy to point the finger, whether or not a particular complaint has merit. Furthermore, when bargaining on wages or prices is limited by government rules the government becomes, in a sense, a third party at the table. Often, a deal wanted by one or even both parties can be gained only by getting government to modify a rule or policy.

The more the government has control over economic affairs, the more there is for interest groups and their representatives to do. Simply to protect its legitimate interests, a group must follow all government regulatory programs affecting its activities, and be prepared to present its case wherever that might be overlooked. And when the prosperity of a group depends largely on government policies and programs, there will be a strong temptation to go beyond mere protection and build up its economic and political power to advance its interests at the expense of other groups. In a rat race, the devil is going to get the hindmost rats—to say nothing of the mice.

When the government controls important economic affairs no one can afford not to belong to a group that can represent him capably; and no group can afford to be weaker than most of the others. Hence, prolonged direct government controls will breed more pressure groups and encourage all these bodies to strive to increase their power.

All this may hurt democracy in several ways.

First, the agencies administering direct control laws will be subjected continuously to "power plays" and pressure tactics to get rulings, exceptions, or changes in policies to benefit particular groups. At the worst this will produce outright corruption. At the least, it is likely to mean occasional favors to powerful groups.

Second, some pressure groups will also try to put into the agencies and the Congress men they can count on for special favors. These groups will be out to "get" the honest administrative officials, senators and congressmen who are trying to serve the general public interest. If perversion of the public interest and corruption become extensive, those who are hurt may lose faith in democracy itself. The year 1951 saw the exposé of graft in government and a general public revulsion against low moral standards in public service. If corruption increased and, in addition, many millions felt that their prices, wages or profits were being held unfairly low by the government while powerful groups got special favors, then faith in democratic government would be seriously impaired.

Continued direct control by government would bring a heightening of intergroup struggle. When individual incomes are vitally affected by government policies, programs and rulings, pressure groups will fight each other through government agencies as well as in the market place and the halls of Congress. Beyond some point group warfare would be a serious threat to democracy, as we noted in the preceding chapter in discussing chronic inflation—which would also heighten group struggle.

Examples of Group Conflicts

Examples of group struggle come readily to mind. As the end of World II came in sight in 1945, various groups redoubled their efforts to win special favors under stabilization controls, or outright release from them. Labor got release from effective wage control immediately after V-J Day. Business and farm groups, feeling that they were being discriminated against, struggled for exemption or weakening of price controls. The corporate excess profits tax was also removed soon after V-J Day, but corporate business apparently feared a squeeze on profit margins from wage increases not matched by ceiling price increases. The result of all this was a series of retreats during 1946, partly by the Administration and partly by the Congress, ending in removal of virtually all price controls in the fall of that year. Labor-management strife also showed itself in a wave of strikes in the first half of 1946.

Another example was the temporary withdrawal of the labor leaders from the Wage Stabilization Board and other defense agencies in February 1951. They protested that the defense program, including direct controls, was being managed with a bias toward business interests.

A recent example is the labor-management struggle in steel in the spring of 1952. First, the collective bargaining process failed over a period of several months to produce a wage contract and settlement of the burning union shop issue. Then the three groups in the Wage Stabilization Board, representing labor, management and the public, failed to reach agreement. The major recommendations, on which the labor and public members agreed, were accepted by the union and denounced by the steel companies, whereupon the union called a strike. Seizure of the steel mills by the President averted the strike but precipitated a legal controversy over the powers of the Executive. After a short interval, the Supreme Court of the United States decided that the seizure was beyond the constitutional power of the President. Thereupon, the mills were returned to the owners, and a strike began which dragged on for two months, in spite of attempts at government mediation. The whole episode is an unhappy but clear example of how government control in the field of wages and industrial relations may reduce the effectiveness of collective bargaining, heighten animosity and intensify economic warfare.

Perils of Political Stalemate

One possible outcome of a sharpened intergroup struggle is political stalemate. This could result from inability of groups to get together in support of positive programs to deal effectively with current problems, with some coalition always able to block most new legislation. The growth in political and economic power of interest groups might even foster a set of splinter parties.

The history of the past fifty years shows that our political system has often tended toward stalemates, at least until there was a crisis, and sometimes even then. It would have been better for the country if the changes in economic institutions made by the New Deal had been spread over the previous fifteen years instead of being compressed into a few years in the middle of the worst depression the country has ever suffered.

In the defense period ahead, our policies should be bold, effective and flexible. We cannot afford a paralyzing stalemate in military policy, in foreign policy or in anti-inflation policy. The dangers of ineffectual efforts in these fields are obvious. It should be just as evident that continued stalemate in the face of these dangers would be an open invitation to a "man on horseback"—a man who could rally support from many of those hurt by inflation and from those fearful of the results of paralysis in the cold war, as well as from the vehement minority who for a variety of reasons unite in desiring a "strong government."

Nor should we shut our eyes to the possibility that two irreconcilable giant coalitions might emerge from the intergroup struggle in a long period of chronic inflationary pressure and extensive direct controls—especially if no relief was in sight from the anxieties and pressures of the cold war. This could lead to a bloodless revolution in which the stronger coalition seized the state, or, perhaps, to civil war. Extremists of the past two decades (other than the Communists) would furnish a core for each coalition. The animosities of the New Deal period have been revived somewhat by the MacArthur episode and the demagogic performance of Senator McCarthy. We Americans are a high-spirited, impetuous people, usually ready to "make something out of it" when we do not like what the other fellow says or does. The troubles, tensions and pressures of the defense period could sort us out into two irreconcilable groups.

The Dilemma—and the Diagnosis Needed

Chronic inflation would damage our economic institutions and threaten democracy itself. Direct controls are at times indispensable to an effective anti-inflation program. But prolonged use of direct controls may also bring undesired changes in our institutions and threaten our democracy.

We need a diagnosis to reveal the conditions under which direct controls are necessary for effective economic mobilization and stabilization, and also the conditions under which we can get rid of them. Unless we can make such a diagnosis, and use it as national policy, we are likely to suffer one of the sets of evils sketched above. Worst of all, we might have chronic inflation simultaneously with direct controls, because of failure to make either direct controls or indirect controls, or both together, strong enough to prevent inflation. This would make disaster almost inevitable.

4. Which to Use—and When

ARE DIRECT CONTROLS NECESSARY some of the time, all the time, or not at all when the defense take is 15, 20 or 25 per cent of national production? If we want to ensure effective mobilization for defense and to curb inflation, we cannot avoid some direct controls some of the time. But we can do without them much of the time, perhaps most of the time, if we use common sense and self-restraint.

Controls on Materials

When a defense program suddenly demands substantial amounts of steel, aluminum, copper, nickel, cobalt or other basic materials, direct controls are needed at first to keep these materials out of unimportant uses and to channel them into defense production, into such defense-supporting activities as transportation, power and plant expansion and into stockpiles if security requires them. That is why some uses of aluminum and copper were prohibited early in the present defense program and why these metals, as well as steel and other materials, were brought under government allocation control in 1951. But why not let defense producers bid the needed supplies away from other users by offering higher prices in the free market? Where the shortage is small and the price would not rise substantially this, of course, would be the wisest policy. But where the shortage is substantial and free market bidding would mean a sharp price increase there are conclusive reasons for controlling directly the use of the material.

Reasons for the Controls

First, there is no assurance that through free market bidding producers of munitions and defense-supporting goods and services and builders of defense plants will actually get the needed quantities of materials on time. At any given moment, suppliers usually have orders on their books for many months ahead. In the absence of government regulations directing them to fill defense orders first, they will probably fill commitments in the order in which these appear on the books. Unless they can increase output considerably or have large stocks on hand, new orders will probably come at the end of the line, regardless of their importance to defense. Moreover, many suppliers are more interested in continuing to serve their regular customers, on whom they depend for sales year in and year out, than in selling to new customers even though these may be defense producers. Thus it may be difficult for defense producers to get their orders accepted, or to get deliveries when needed, unless the government requires that priority be given to deliveries to defense producers or allocates the supply of the material.

Second, if free market bidding for materials pushed prices to levels yielding more than reasonable returns, the cost of munitions and other defense goods would be raised unnecessarily.[1] This would also make it more difficult to balance the budget, since that would require further tax increases.

Third, if the profits of materials producers rose sharply as a result of price increases, labor would probably demand and receive substantial wage increases. Wage increases in basic materials would tend to spread and to feed inflation.

---

1. Demands for basic materials in many uses are quite "inelastic"—that is, a substantial rise in price does not cause much reduction in the amounts demanded by manufacturers, processors or builders.

Decontrol When Supply Increases

In the early stages of a defense program direct controls on the uses of some materials are needed, for the reasons just given. However, when the supply of a material can be enlarged to cover all or nearly all civilian demands as well as all defense demands, these direct controls will no longer be needed. If total defense demand drops after a time, that will usually make it easier to balance capacity and demand so that the controls can be lifted.

Suppose the defense take of steel reaches its peak in 1953 and then levels off to a plateau. Sooner or later, steel capacity (plant and manpower) can be increased to meet all civilian demands for steel in autos, building construction, hardware and other things as well as all defense needs. This can be done, roughly at least, for each kind of alloy steel as well as for the common carbon steel, and for all the different forms or shapes, such as sheets, rails, pipe, beams, girders, etc. Perhaps this balance between capacity and demand could be reached by 1953 or 1954.[2] At any rate the balance could come as soon thereafter as new steel furnaces and finishing mills could be built and arrangements made to enlarge the flow of iron ore from the mines. Then allocation of steel could be removed.

In a few cases, adequate increase in supply of a particular material may require several years. Known reserves of some minerals are quite limited and exploration takes time and may not bring in substantial new ore bodies. Also, some im-

2. Demand, as used here, means, of course, the amount demanded at a specific price. When we speak of balance of capacity and demand for a material in the next few pages, demand should be understood to mean the amount demanded at a price that would yield to producers the ordinary returns received in years of general prosperity that are free both from general inflation and from the distortions of demand for particular things that come with a substantial defense program.

ported materials, such as natural rubber and nickel, are under tight foreign control. Copper seems to be an example of both cases. In 1951, it was estimated that the copper supply available to this country, including imports, could be increased in a few years by not more than 15 per cent above the 1950 level.[3] In the few cases where supplies cannot be expanded enough, allocation or some other control on use may have to be maintained for many years, if defense demands continue to exhaust a substantial part of the limited supply.

But the steel case seems to be more typical. Given a few years, supplies of most materials (in larger demand because of the defense programs) can probably be increased enough to permit the removal of controls on their use. Of course, construction of new facilities or exploration and development of mineral reserves may at times take longer than usual because needed materials or manpower cannot be spared immediately from current defense production or defense "tooling up." And success in curbing inflation may also require slower expansion of capacity using short materials. But this is the point: within a few years, supply can catch up and controls be removed, if the total of defense and civilian demand stays on a plateau, or rises only at a slow normal growth that can be matched by growth of capacity—a "rising plateau."

Humps in Defense Take and Demand for Materials

Defense demand for some materials may not stay on a plateau after 1953 or 1954. Suppose the defense demand for steel falls in the years 1955-1957 to a level well below the peak 1952-1953, and then jumps in 1958-1960 to a similar peak. Controls will probably not be needed while defense

3. Council of Economic Advisers, *The Economic Situation at Midyear 1951*, p. 85.

demand is low. If growth of steel capacity during or after the first hump is big enough, allocation will not be needed in the second hump, provided always that the mills can obtain sufficient manpower for capacity output.[4] Otherwise, allocation will be necessary until demand again falls off or capacity catches up.

A jump in defense demand for steel might reflect simply a shift to more steel-using armament. But it might be part of another general defense build-up like that of 1950-1953.

Should we have a succession of humps and troughs in total defense take during the next two decades, would it be necessary to restore controls on materials in every hump? Not if civilian demand for materials dropped as defense demands rose, preventing peaks in total civilian and defense demand. But this will not happen of its own accord. A sharp rise in defense demand usually will accelerate total demand. With the increase in defense demand, more people will be employed and there will be more money to spend; hence retail sales will rise. Manufacturers will want to expand output of consumer goods and some will want to add plant and machinery for this purpose. Retailers may want to put up new stores or enlarge old ones. The demand for materials for civilian use is in fact likely to increase during the hump— as it did in 1950-1951.

Curbs on Civilian Demand

Total consumer and business demand in the civilian area can and should be held down in defense humps by tax increases and drastic curbs on credit. These measures would

4. This does not imply that it would be wise to increase capacity to meet hump demands. (See the next section of this chapter.) Moreover, it is unlikely that capacity for every type or form of steel would have been increased just enough to meet the new hump demand, so allocation might be needed on some particular steel products.

reduce the number of materials requiring direct controls. But even if fiscal and credit measures were strong enough to reduce *total* civilian demand (consumer plus business) while defense demand rose, demand for some materials heavily used in defense production would still increase so much in relation to available supplies that direct controls would be necessary to ensure sufficient, appropriate and timely supplies to defense producers.

Government could also help reduce the extent and duration of direct controls on use of materials in defense humps if it could cut substantially nondefense projects using scarce materials—e.g., government buildings and power and flood control projects—pushing these ahead faster in the troughs. This expedient, however, is not a major reed. Once such projects are under way, it is often wasteful to halt or slow operations. Variation in the rate of operation is much more feasible in highway construction and other so-called "light" public works—but these are largely in the domain of state and local governments, which tend to increase such programs during booms and slow them down in business recessions. Perhaps the federal government could modify this through its grant-in-aid policy.[5]

The federal government could also reduce somewhat the need for direct controls on use of materials in the humps by buying for reserve stocks in interim periods when capacity output was not otherwise being taken. This is feasible if a material can be stored in standard forms, alloys or compounds that will keep and that can be converted readily into

5. It may be noted that anything which postpones demand for building construction, housing, public works or consumer durable goods from the defense hump to the trough would have two advantages in addition to lessening the need for direct controls on materials during the hump: (1) it would help prevent or lessen inflation during the hump, and (2) it would help prevent or lessen business recession during the defense trough.

those needed as types and designs of weapons change. This is the case with many metals, such as copper, aluminum, zinc and lead.

However, this cannot entirely avoid the necessity for direct controls in humps. For some materials it is not feasible; and for others there is no guarantee that sufficiently large reserve stocks can be built up between humps.

Capacities Geared to Hump Demands?

The only sure way to avoid the need for direct controls on use of some materials during hump periods would be to expand capacities for all materials enough so that they could meet the peak demands (civilian plus defense)—if we knew beforehand what those demands would be! Even if we could do this, would it be wise?

Certainly not in the case of those materials for which demand would climb for two or three years, and then fall off markedly for three, five or seven years. It would be wasteful to build a lot of steel or aluminum plants that would be used only a fraction of the time—particularly when we could never know whether the fraction would be one half or one fifth or one tenth! Probably we shall have to put more effort into defense than we like in coming years, but we do not have to add to this needlessly.

The steel required to build enough steel plant capacity to carry the peaks of total demand for steel can, together with other materials, make a lot of automobiles, schools and theaters.

Balancing Supplies and "Regular" Demands

It makes more sense to try to adjust capacity for each material to the best possible estimates of "regular" defense demand between humps plus "regular" civilian demand, with allowance for the normal peacetime growth in civilian demand. "Regular" demand (defense or civilian) means the level likely to prevail in between-hump periods, neglecting minor year-to-year variations, and assuming general prosperity without inflation.[6] This notion of "regular" demand can be applied to defense demand for a material only if the defense authorities "plan it that way"—that is, make plans for a fairly level defense take of the material in the period between humps. We shall come back to this point soon.

Balancing productive capacities of most materials against "regular" demands of a between-hump period means that direct controls on the use of many materials will be needed during the humps of demand. But it can and should be recognized that such use can be temporary and that controls can be removed in each case as soon as there is a balance of demand and production. Moreover, as we saw above, the number of materials needing control and the duration of their control can be lessened by strong fiscal and credit policies, by curtailment in the hump of some government programs using materials in demand for defense, and by building reserve stocks of some materials in trough periods.

Is it practicable to try to balance capacities against demands so that in general controls on use of materials can in most cases be confined to a hump or to a build-up to a new plateau? The answer is "Yes," if defense authorities will make careful plans for a steady (or tapering) defense take for a period of four or five years after a hump or build-up and stick to these plans, apart from sudden, radical innovations

6. To repeat, demand, as here used, means the amount that will be purchased at prices yielding the ordinary returns of peacetime general prosperity without inflation.

in weapons or a major new emergency.[7] Estimating "regular" civilian demand for a material is not an exact science, but it can probably be done well enough to make it possible to apply the policy of balancing capacity and demand with fair success if the "regular" defense demand is known and steady. But this policy cannot work if defense authorities do not make estimates for several years ahead, if the estimates are faulty, or if the plans call for sharp fluctuations in the defense take between humps.

Of course, if it is clear that the needed supply of a material in full war (including minimum essential civilian use) will exceed the "regular" defense and civilian demand, its capacity should be geared to the war level.

Aids to Expansion of Capacity

Will business automatically expand output capacity to keep materials up to the levels of these "regular" demands? Not in cases where businessmen are afraid that defense demand or civilian demand will actually be less than official estimates. But government can do a lot to promote needed expansion through overcoming such fears by making reliable estimates and by sharing the risks or assuming them itself.

First, government can work out careful, scientific estimates through its production programming—that is, scheduling the needed output of military products and the corresponding requirements of materials and parts, and estimating the civilian demands for these materials.[8]

Second, "accelerated amortization" for tax purposes can be allowed when business adds new facilities to meet defense

7. A moderate drop in defense take below the estimate would obviously do no harm, unless followed in a year or so by a jump above the original estimate.

8. Production programming is described in Chapter 5.

needs and pays for them with its own money. This is the way it works:

The XYZ Steel Company builds new blast furnaces and open-hearth furnaces at a cost of $30 million. Under the ordinary tax rules the company could deduct from income as amortization cost (depreciation of the facilities) only a small amount each year—say 4 per cent of the $30 million investment, if the tax authorities ruled the ordinary useful life of such facilities to be twenty-five years. With accelerated amortization, the company is allowed to deduct as depreciation cost each year 20 per cent of the $30 million. In five years, the company will have recovered out of sales revenue its $30 million investment, with a profit to boot—if a profitable defense demand for the full product of the new steel furnaces lasts for five years.

This plan for rapid write-offs of new plant needed for defense was used in World War II and it has been revived in the present defense program. It is, of course, a scheme to induce private business to bear much of the investment cost of the extra plant and equipment needed to meet defense demand, over and above regular civilian demand. If the large defense demand were almost sure to last for ten to fifteen years this scheme would probably not be needed to induce businesses to put in enough new investment in basic materials capacity to meet expected regular defense and civilian demand. But, of course, no one can know whether a large defense program will be needed for more than a few years. So business can hardly be expected to invest heavily in plant that might turn out to be pretty much of a loss unless a rapid write-off were permitted.[9]

9. At the end of 1952 accelerated tax amortization had been approved by the Defense Production Administrator for $14.5 billion of projected plant

Third, there are other means by which government can share with business the risks of overexpanded facilities: loans or loan guarantees on appropriate terms, or long-term purchase contracts. All these measures are being used in the present defense program.

Finally, government can build plant at public expense if business cannot be induced to expand capacity to meet regular defense and civilian demand. Government plant can be leased to private operators or operated by government. In the case of most basic materials, leasing to private operators on reasonable terms probably is the more desirable. It is difficult to achieve a satisfactory mixture of private and government operation in the same market. And it probably is not wise to try too many experiments that would change our economic or political institutions in this trying period.

The aims of this country's present defense program seem to have been in line with those sketched above. Large increases in capacity have been encouraged in steel, aluminum, chemicals, petroleum, electric power, rail transport and many other industries.[10] Top defense officials have looked forward to lifting most controls on use of materials after these expansion programs were completed and defense demand leveled off or dropped back somewhat in 1953 or 1954.

------

investment found by the Administrator to be attributable to defense purposes. This represented about three fifths of the total cost of these plants estimated at $25 billion, of which about 35 per cent was to be in place by the end of 1953. *Eighth Quarterly Report of the Director of Defense Mobilization,* January 1, 1953, p. 19. There has been some criticism that the authorities have been lax in granting the rapid write-off for such a large amount of new investment. The author has not attempted to make an appraisal on this difficult question.

10. *Second Quarterly Report of the Director of Defense Mobilization,* July 1, 1951, pp. 11 ff., and later quarterly reports.

General Inflationary Pressure Must Be Eased

This book has emphasized the belief that allocations and other controls on uses of materials can be dropped after supplies of these goods have been expanded enough to cover total demands—civilian plus defense. We must recognize, however, that adequate *physical* expansion of supplies is not, in itself, sufficient to bring about this condition. Total civilian demand of the whole economy must be so limited by fiscal and credit controls or other measures that the sum of civilian and government demand does not exceed the value of the output of the economy at stable prices.

If government is using deficit financing to swing its defense buying and if banks are extending credit freely in large amounts, then consumers, business and government all will be trying to buy more than the available supply of goods and services. Inflationary pressure will be general. All the most needed materials will be in short supply. If controls on their use were lifted, the defense program might not get everything needed in spite of expanded capacities and some decline in defense demands. Thus it is clear that strong fiscal and credit controls are necessary for removal of controls on use of materials as well as to prevent or minimize inflation.

In general, these principles apply also to facilities and manpower. But there are important differences in practice. A primary aim of the present defense program is to build new capacity for military products instead of converting civilian goods plants, as we did in World War II. At present, direct control of use of facilities plays a small part.

Incentive Controls for Manpower

In the case of manpower, there is another difference. Manpower shortages have appeared in some localities. And some skilled workers, such as tool and die makers, have been scarce almost everywhere. More shortages may appear as the new defense plants go into operation. But even if manpower shortages should become very troublesome, we probably shall not go in for mandatory assignment of particular persons to particular jobs (except in the armed forces), comparable to mandatory allocations of steel, aluminum and copper. Assignment of workers to different jobs in other localities is obviously a much greater interference with human lives than is the interference with business management that goes with assignment of more copper to electronics and cartridge brass, and less to ash trays and kitchen and bathroom water pipe.

Many kinds of incentive control can help meet manpower needs in defense production—good wages and working conditions, assurance of overtime work, provision of adequate community facilities, such as schools and playgrounds, training programs, and occupational deferment—supplemented by more active employment services and voluntary control of labor pirating. These measures to allocate labor and to increase the supplies of particular skills are not repugnant to our basic values and institutions, and many of them may be of value in ordinary peacetime. But even these controls can be reduced as manpower shortages are overcome.

Hence we may conclude that—given time—supplies of most materials, facilities and kinds of manpower can be expanded, and direct controls on their use dropped, as supply comes into line with demand, provided always that fiscal and credit controls curb general inflationary pressure. *Direct controls on use of materials, facilities and manpower can be confined pretty much to hump periods if we sufficiently expand supplies and maintain strong fiscal and credit controls.*

Price Ceilings Needed with Allocations and Priorities

When deliveries of a certain material are regulated by government allocation or by priority orders, a government price ceiling is usually needed for two reasons: (1) to be sure that buyers—including the government, which is the ultimate buyer when the material goes into military products —are not charged unreasonable prices; and (2) to help make the allocation or priority order work well.

To Ensure Reasonable Prices

Allocation or priority orders are needed only when total demand for a material is much greater than available supply, at the going price. This means that many users would be willing to pay a much higher price—particularly those who could pass on the increase to the government or to other buyers of their products. Procurement officers purchasing planes, tanks, guns and ammunition cannot control the prices of aluminum, steel, copper and chemicals charged to makers of these items. And in such a "sellers' market," the auto makers and farm equipment manufacturers cannot have much to say about the price of steel. Only government ceiling prices can ensure reasonable prices for materials in heavy defense demand.[11]

To Help Make the Orders Work

Allocation or priority orders do not automatically work

11. It is sometimes said that allocation orders or other controls on use of materials will in themselves control prices because they cut demand down exactly to the available supply. This might happen in some cases, but it certainly would not in others where all or most of the buyers could pass on to their customers higher materials costs. In such a case, a high price could be obtained—and a small overissue of allocation claims could lead to a very big jump in price. This is a complex matter in which it would be foolish to rely on simple theories or guesses on the results. Clearly, it is much harder for government to lower prices than to keep them from rising.

well. Price ceilings on materials subject to such orders can help make them function in two ways:

1. If there is no legal maximum price there will be a great temptation to violate the allocation or priority order, by serving customers eager to pay high prices. It is hard enough in any case to deny favors to old customers or to promising new customers.

2. Unless government sets a ceiling, there may not be a recognized uniform price for the material. With every part of the supply under allocation or priorities there can be no competitive bidding for the material. Hence there will be no price automatically decided by the market. If government does not set a ceiling, there may be many different prices. If allocation or priorities cover only a part of the supply of a material, the same might be true for that part—and to make matters worse, competitive bidding for the "open end" might drive the price there quite high. Would this also be the price for the supplies delivered on government order? Where large firms are accustomed to set prices for a material, they sometimes set different prices. For example, the custom smelters of copper sometimes charge a higher price than other refiners. If this happened with copper under allocation, would government have to decide which users had to pay the higher price? Government allocation of a material to different users at different prices may not be impossible, but it seems obvious that allocation will work much better with uniform government ceiling prices.

Ceiling prices to accompany allocation or priority orders can be removed when the controls on materials are lifted. If there were no other reasons for ceiling price control, we could end our discussion of it here. But there are circumstances in which general price and wage controls are needed as complements of fiscal and credit controls.

Why Selective Wage Control Is Impracticable

There might seem to be a parallel case for wage control in industries producing materials scarce enough to need both control of their use and price ceilings. But wage rates in these industries obviously should not be held below the general trend. And as a practical matter it is doubtful whether government can impose wage control on a few unions and leave others free from control—unless these others cannot, in fact, secure wage increases because of soft markets for the goods they produce. Most of those familiar with wage problems agree that if formal wage control is used, as a rule, it must go across the board. Of course, the government may be able to influence particular wage bargains between big unions and big corporations by "jawbone control." If this does not work and if there is a prospect that large wage increases in some industries will set off a general "round" of inflationary wage boosts, across-the-board wage control is needed. This brings us to the problem of general price and wage ceilings.

General Price and Wage Controls

At all times fiscal and credit controls are the "iron men on the stabilization team, and especially in a limited defense program. We must use them effectively every month and every year, varying their strength with changes in the economic situation. If we do this, general price and wage controls will not be needed all the time and they may not be needed most of the time.

Why are they needed at all?

Because there are some inflationary forces—not only economic but also psychological and political—with which fiscal and credit measures cannot always deal satisfactorily. These are speculative and panic buying and the forces of a self-propelling spiral of prices and wages. Direct controls may also be needed to hold down prices and wages if there should be a short period of deficit financing at a peak of defense expenditures.

To Stem Panic Buying

In the months following the outbreak in Korea, June 1950, we saw a quick surge of panic and speculative buying. This was a chief reason for the sharp price increases that summer and fall.

With actual fighting in Korea there was the possibility of imminent world war and the certainty of a big jump in military expenditures, even before the exact scale of the defense program became known. People remembered the shortages and the price increases in World War II. Individuals rushed to buy automobiles, television sets, refrigerators, tires, clothing, sugar and many other things. Businesses rushed to build up inventories of materials and to buy equipment or arrange for plant expansion before restrictions came on or before prices went up. A lull in spending in the fall was followed by another buying surge after the Chinese Communists went into Korea, late in November.

A large part of the "hurry-scurry" buying was financed by new borrowing from the banks. Between the end of May 1950 (the month before the Korean outbreak) and the end of December of that year, total loans of all commercial banks in the country increased by about $8 billion and the volume

TABLE 3

COMMERCIAL BANK LOANS AND DEPOSITS AND
CURRENCY, MAY 1950 AND DECEMBER 1950
(*In Billions of Dollars*)

Item	End of May 1950	End of December 1950	Increase
Total bank loans	$ 44.1	$ 52.2	$8.1
Total deposits and currency outside banks	173.0	180.6	7.6
Total deposits and currency (outside banks) excluding government deposits	169.2	176.9	7.7

Source: Council of Economic Advisers, *Annual Economic Review,* January 1952, pp. 193-94 (data from Board of Governors of the Federal Reserve System).

Comparisons between May 1950 and March 1951, the peak of wholesale prices, are difficult to interpret because of the large seasonal increase in government deposits on account of tax receipts.

of deposits and currency (outside banks) grew by almost the same figure. (See Table 3.)

The spending of savings or of idle balances of individuals and businesses was also an important factor in the increased buying. Between the second quarter of 1950 and the first quarter of 1951 the value of the total national product grew from $275 billion to $319 billion, an increase of 16 per cent. In the same period the total of privately owned deposits and currency outside banks rose from $110 billion to $115 billion or an increase of less than 5 per cent.[12] Evidently individual and business spending of deposits and currency was speeded up. The same thing is indicated by the estimates of personal saving given in Table 4.

The Start of a Buying Spree

A surge of speculative or scare buying can occur with any

12. Council of Economic Advisers, *Annual Economic Review,* January 1952, pp. 167 and 194. Privately owned deposits means total deposits less government deposits. From the second quarter of 1950 to the second quarter of 1951 the value of the national product increased by 19 per cent while the increase in the "money supply," as used here, was still less than 5 per cent.

TABLE 4

ESTIMATES OF PERSONAL SAVINGS, 1950-1951

Period	Personal Net Saving (In Billions of Dollars, Annual Rate Seasonally Adjusted)	Net Saving as Percentage of Disposable Personal Income
1950 First quarter	$12.5	6.3
Second quarter	8.9	4.5
Third quarter	4.6	2.2
Fourth quarter	16.8	7.8
1951 First quarter	8.5	3.9
Second quarter	20.1	9.1
Third quarter	22.2	9.9
Fourth quarter	23.0	10.1

Source: Council of Economic Advisers, *Annual Economic Review,* January 1952, p. 175 (data from Department of Commerce).

Note: The estimates of personal net saving are the difference between disposable personal income (personal income less taxes) and consumption expenditures. Spending of past savings obviously tends to reduce the margin between disposable income and expenditures.

sudden change in the outlook, reflecting the start of another large defense build-up, the imminent danger of war, or both. Individuals and businesses have large financial resources to use in a buying spree—the so-called "liquid assets," which include cash balances, savings accounts, and holdings of bonds and other easily salable securities.

Perhaps another Korea would not be accompanied by such speculative or scare buying. In 1950 and 1951, fear of severe shortages proved groundless, and after their sharp increases a number of prices receded somewhat in 1951. However, the average of consumer prices continued to rise through 1951 and much of 1952 and the average of wholesale prices remained almost 10 per cent above pre-Korean levels. If the popular reaction usually reflects the most recent comparable experience, another Korea would not set off as large a wave of increased buying, but there would probably be some increase in anticipation of higher prices. In any case, predictions are likely to prove unreliable, and we should be prepared to curb a surge of speculative or panic buying whenever it occurs.

A big jump in personal income tax rates and corporate profit tax rates, a sharp, swift contraction of bank credit, or a combination of these, could scotch inflation with the first surge of speculative or scare buying. In practice, however, it is doubtful whether taxes can be increased speedily enough to counteract a buying wave; and credit contraction severe enough to do the job might produce a panic or a recession or both.

Congressional hearings and debate on a new bill to increase tax rates usually last months rather than days. The only effective way to counter scare buying with tax increases would be enactment by Congress of an emergency schedule of temporary rate increases to go into effect automatically on a declaration by the President that it was needed to combat inflation or on the passage of a joint resolution by Congress. Probably Congress would be less inclined to give this power to the President than to give him stand-by-power to use price and wage controls in a sudden inflationary emergency. It is also questionable whether Congress itself would rush into effect a schedule previously enacted. Moreover, it would be impossible to know how large an increase in tax receipts would be needed to offset a future buying surge of unknown size.

A Clamp on Credit Expansion

At the first sign of a wave of speculative or scare buying the Federal Reserve should take immediate measures stiff enough to prevent any further expansion of bank credit at all, except where that was needed for the defense program or for other highly essential uses, such as completion of a partly built hospital. Such a clamp on credit expansion would make it impossible for most individuals and businesses to borrow more. It might also discourage much spending of idle balances or savings—by diminishing the inflationary psychology and by serving notice that spenders could not borrow from the banks to replace used balances or savings. Credit policy of this sort might prevent inflation entirely or hold it to a tolerable minimum so that direct controls would not be needed.

Resort to Credit Contraction?

However, this might not always be the result. If strong inflationary psychology caused large spending of balances and savings, even with a clamp on credit expansion, then only a substantial *contraction* of credit outstanding would prevent inflation. This would mean that banks would have to call loans or refuse to renew them, in part or in whole, when they came due.

General contraction of credit might prove highly unsatisfactory. The amount of added spending of liquid assets per month or per quarter could never be estimated even approximately, so it would be impossible to know how much credit contraction would be needed to avoid inflation. In practice, the amount of contraction usually would be too little or too much. Faced with an explosion of buying, credit authorities could not feel their way by gradual adjustments as in ordinary times. To be sure to prevent inflation they would have to be drastic. This might produce a panic, as securities were dumped or funds withdrawn to repay loans or to meet commitments for which borrowing had been planned. Or the drastic credit contraction might produce business recession and unemployment, even in the face of a prospective defense build-up.

A General Wage-Price Freeze

On the other hand, a general freeze of prices and wages across the board is a neat instrument for dealing with a spending wave. Congress willing, it can at one stroke nip in the bud or slow a general price rise, without harsh effects on business and employment. Of course, a freeze will bring some inequities and some "squeezes" that would hurt production, but these can soon be removed by adjustments.

To be in a position to apply a freeze quickly and to administer it effectively the government must have continuous authority for price and wage control and must keep on the job a staff nucleus with plans for rapid expansion to an operating basis. One reason for this is the fact that a buying spurt can start almost overnight. There is an additional reason: if a freeze is expected both businesses and unions will try to raise their prices before it occurs. They probably will not be deterred by the thought of rollbacks, which experience has shown to be unlikely.

After a few months, several months or, perhaps, a year the inflationary psychology producing a buying surge will usually subside if the immediate war scare or other cause fades, if people see that shortages are not likely to be as large or as imminent as they had feared and if both direct and indirect controls have dissipated the fears of inflation. General price and wage controls then can be removed (unless they are needed to curb an inflationary spiral) provided increased tax rates and stronger credit restrictions made in the meantime suffice to hold down total civilian demand to the available supply of goods for civilians at steady prices.

Even after the scare buying disappears most people and businesses may want to spend a larger part of their incomes than usual (or even dip deeper into savings) in a period in which rising defense expenditure results in a continuing inflationary psychology. But given time, tax increases and credit restrictions can probably be effected to offset or curb this extra spending, which will be far smaller than the surge of speculative or scare buying.

It is often argued, and with reason, that no harm is done if prices go up 5 or 10 per cent in a wave of scare buying and then fall back to their previous level, or close to it. But after a 5 or 10 per cent rise, will prices come down to the former level? The increase may start a price-wage spiral; or wage increases may produce a "ratchet" effect that keeps prices from falling to previous levels, or near them.

To Hold Prices in a Short Spending Peak

General price and wage controls may also be needed to prevent inflation during a short peak of defense expenditure accompanied by a substantial budget deficit. If defense spending is to peak up sharply for ten to fifteen months, and then fall back, it probably will be neither practicable nor desirable to raise tax rates or to cut other government spending simply to cover this peak of defense spending.

The temporary government deficit would not produce general inflationary pressure if offset by extra sales of bonds to individuals and businesses, with their spending cut by the amount of these extra bond purchases. Savings will probably increase somewhat at a time when direct controls on materials reduce the supplies of consumer durables and plant equipment and the number of houses, factories and stores that can be built. This tendency can be increased if the government convinces the public that after a year or two the production of consumer durable goods, houses, plant and equipment will be resumed.

Tighter restrictions on credit for general business use, on installment buying, and on housing loans should be a primary means of trying to offset the inflationary effects of the temporary deficit, even at the risk of brief adverse effects on business volume and on employment.

Unless a price-wage spiral was churning, a combination of more saving and less credit might serve to prevent inflation through the peak of defense spending. But it is impossible to predict in advance how much extra saving can be obtained or the precise effects of the credit restrictions.

If general price and wage controls are already in effect it would be only prudent to continue them through a short defense peak. If not already in effect, direct controls might need to be invoked—in the form of a temporary general freeze—to check a spiral of price and wage increases which could not be halted by other measures. However, price ceilings at certain strategic points might possibly be sufficient to check the spiral.

Chapter 2 emphasized the dangers of trying to repress inflation by price and wage controls over a long period in which total demand constantly outruns total supply, and savings pile up. However, unless the deficit is very large, these dangers will not be serious in a short period of several months or a year or two. If spiraling forces would turn a little inflation, resulting from temporary deficit financing, into a lot of inflation it is doubly important to repress it.[13]

13. This was pointed out by J. K. Galbraith in "The Strategy of Direct Control in Economic Mobilization," *Review of Economics and Statistics*, February 1951, p. 12.
The term "repressed" rather than the more common "suppressed" inflation

To Halt a Spiral of Prices and Wages

Fiscal and credit controls tight enough to prevent the appearance of a general inflationary gap between total demand and total supply will not necessarily curb inflation. Indirect controls limit total demand but they cannot prevent price or wage increases at specific points, any more than they can prevent or break bottlenecks at specific points.

Increases in some prices or some wage rates may set off a self-propelling spiral of rising prices and wage rates. We have a self-propelling spiral when increases in some particular prices or wage rates induce rises elsewhere which, in turn, touch off additional increases. Sooner or later this chain reaction returns to the starting points and they "get into the act" for a second round.

How the Spiral Operates

The spiral operates through interaction of "cost push" and "demand pull," to use the graphic terms of Albert Hart.[14] Higher prices of materials or higher wage rates lead manufacturers to raise the prices of finished goods. Wholesalers and retailers, faced with these higher prices, in turn raise their selling prices to maintain their usual percentage markups.

Price and wage increases raise incomes in many, if not most, cases. When the price of a product goes up its total sales revenue increases, unless the volume sold falls by more than the price rise—not a widespread result when demand in gen-

---

is used here as in Albert G. Hart, *Defense without Inflation*. Professor Fritz Machlup notes that Professor Röpke, who is credited with the concept, preferred the English word "repress" because it does not connote finality, as does "suppress." *Review of Economics and Statistics*, August 1949, p. 210.

14. *Defense without Inflation*, Chapter 4.

eral is buoyant. Thus spendable income increases, however it may be split between profits and wages in the industry, or between this particular industry and its suppliers. Wage increases, of course, raise the spendable income of workers, except in the infrequent case where output and employment are substantially cut back.

Hence price and wage increases, if they are fairly general, tend to promote the increases in income and spending to pay for them. Of course, some expansion of bank credit usually will be required to finance business operations at the higher level of costs, but the credit increase merely follows and facilitates the primary spiraling forces.

The spiral also operates partly through various kinds of psychological and political tie-up between different prices or different wages. Thus an increase in the price of steel may lead to price boosts on other materials because steel is considered a bellwether. A jump in the prices of important cost-of-living items such as rent, fuel, meat or milk may lead to demands for wage raises.

A rise in wage rates in steel, automobiles, electrical equipment or rubber is likely to lead to demands for wage increases in other industries, unless it is recognized as an increase to "catch up" on the current round. This is partly psychological but it is also partly political. Unions are in fact political bodies. Their leaders find it hard to stay in office, especially in a union that is governed democratically, unless they can deliver at least part of what the leaders of other unions are getting for their members.

Interacting ties that propel the spiral increasingly have been put into laws and contracts. The law requires that prices of a number of farm products be supported by government at levels based on the parity formula, a relationship between prices paid by farmers for what they buy and prices received by farmers for what they sell. We noted earlier that many wage contracts have escalator clauses under which wage rates change automatically with changes in the Bureau of Labor Statistics consumers' price index.

How a Spiral Starts

There are several ways in which a self-propelling spiral of price and wage increases may start. Increases resulting from panic buying may launch it. If general price and wage controls are not applied quickly enough to stop the panic buying early, they may be needed for a longer time, in order to halt the spiral.

Even without panic buying a spiral may start simply from increases in prices and wages in industries producing materials, equipment and services in specially heavy demand in the first part of a defense build-up—metals, chemicals, machine tools, electronics, etc. Unorganized as well as organized labor in these fields can get wage increases.

Government spending itself may not expand rapidly for a year or two. It takes time for industry to "tool up" for large production of munitions; meanwhile business is spending money in this process of getting ready. Private business dollars spent on machinery and filling the "pipelines" with adequate inventories of materials are just as inflationary as government spending. The same is true for business spending on new defense plants, as in 1940-1942 and 1950-1952. After the large plant expansion of 1950-1952 defense humps in later years might not require nearly so much extension of plant capacity or of equipment. But we cannot be sure of this. Changes in weapons may call for extensive new equipment, and plant dispersal would require much new plant.

If there were no problem of wage increases, price increases on key materials caused by business expenditures for tooling up and for defense output or new plants could be handled by price ceilings on these materials, without general price control. But there probably will be a problem of wage increases, unless we go into a defense build-up from a semi-depressed condition as we did in 1940. Even in the spring of 1941, with several million still unemployed, wage rates started to go up ahead of consumer prices. As we have seen, wage control, to be effective, has to be fairly general, and general wage control, to be acceptable to labor, probably has to be accompanied by general price control.

A Spiral May Start by Anticipation of Demand

We have been talking so far about price and wage increases that resulted more or less automatically from the pull of large increases in demand for materials. But in cases like many of the metals which have prices set by administrative action of business managements, price advances might occur even before the increase in demand—that is, in anticipation of the increase. This would start the spiral sooner. It is also true, of course, that these "administered" price increases might not come until later, thus slowing up the beginnings of a spiral.

The same is true of wage rates in fields where there are strong unions. The unions may demand substantial wage advances in anticipation of large defense spending, manpower shortages and a potential rise in living costs. On the other hand, they may show restraint, waiting to see whether shortages actually develop or living costs jump. An existing labor contract, of course, may make it impossible for a union to bring up the question of raising wage rates for several months. Some contracts, however, have wage reopening clauses. Moreover, after the Korean outbreak we saw that some business managements were glad to have an immediate wage advance—evidently to protect their labor supply—even though their contracts contained no reopening clause. Managements also may raise the wages of unorganized labor for the same reason.

A price-wage spiral can start in the area of materials important for defense uses even though there is no inflationary gap in the economy as a whole. Once started, the spiral will spread. Higher costs of these materials will push up prices of consumer and capital goods made from them. Wage advances in the defense materials field will generate wage advances elsewhere. Individuals with larger wage or profit incomes will spend more. This will pull up prices of foods, clothing items and other "soft goods," thus raising the cost of living.

The spiral *could* start outside the defense materials area; but there are sure to be price and wage increases within that field, unless they are restrained by direct controls. In practice there will also be increases elsewhere if business and labor leaders expect some inflation—especially if they think there will be a freeze of prices and wages after a measure of inflation has occurred. The greater the number who try to get ahead of inflation, or even to keep pace with it, the faster the spiral will spin. With a freeze in the offing, nobody wants to be "caught with his prices down"—and the same for wages.

We saw the spiral at work in 1941-1943, and again after the war, although in the years 1946-1948 the excess money supply resulting from the war finance and the pent-up demands created a kind of forced draft. More recently, the summer and winter of 1950 exhibited an inflationary spiral at work. At that time, there was no general inflationary gap resulting from a federal deficit. On the contrary, there was a cash surplus in the budget in nearly every month of the second half of 1950. An expansion of bank deposits of about $7 billion from June to December 1950 unquestionably helped the spiral. But part of this expansion of bank credit simply *followed* the increases in prices and wages, and probably would not have occurred had they not occurred.

Fiscal and Credit Measures Inadequate by Themselves

Perhaps fiscal and credit controls could overcome a very mild, slow-moving spiral. But the important question is: can they by themselves control a surging spiral?

To curb a spiral, indirect controls would have to deter businessmen and workers from making price and wage increases. Once these increases take place, indirect controls, speaking practically, cannot roll them back!

In industries making munitions or materials and parts for munitions, businessmen and workers know that they can get price and wage increases, which will be passed on to the government, without any cut in volume. Even if all businessmen, labor leaders and workers were convinced that every year or half year taxes would be increased as quickly and as often as was necessary to keep the federal cash budget balanced (or even to keep a certain minimum surplus), they would not for that reason forego price and wage increases. Speaking generally, the individual business or union could not prevent other price or wage increases—and hence the tax rise—by giving up an advance in its own prices or wages.[15] Hence a tight fiscal policy cannot prevent a spiral

15. The policies of some individual corporations and unions influence the policies of others. If all of these price and wage "leaders" refrained from increases, that could have an important general effect.

in the defense industries, and a spiral starting there will spread.

Credit controls can eliminate some of the "demand pull" and modify inflationary psychology, thus helping materially to control the spiral. Credit control could also prevent specific price and wage advances if it could deprive businesses of funds to pay the higher material and labor costs. If business enterprises using bank credit for working capital really believed that the banks would not increase their credit as material costs and wage costs rose, they would try to resist price and wage increases, wherever possible. But would the banks encourage them to believe that credit rationing would be as tough as this, or show by example that it would be?

In practice, most businesses cannot prevent increases in the prices of their materials, and many cannot prevent wage advances. And once wage increases are embodied in a wage contract they cannot be rescinded because of inability to get credit, even if they could have been prevented. Furthermore, banks that refused to finance larger working capital needs of successful firms would be foregoing profits on perfectly sound loans. Even a very tight Federal Reserve policy would not make it certain that banks would refuse additional credit to sound businesses to finance operations at higher costs. They might curtail credit elsewhere.

All this is particularly true in the case of defense contractors. Tough credit restrictions would not be allowed to slow up the production and delivery of munitions. If defense contractors could not get adequate credit from the banks, they would obtain it from the government in advances on their contracts or in some other form. Furthermore, many corporations have their own working capital accumulated out of past profits or realized from the sale of securities.

It seems clear that fiscal and credit controls cannot keep particular price and wage advances from setting off a spiral and helping to keep it going—unless the indirect controls are so drastic as to produce a marked recession and dim the business outlook in the nondefense area. With excess capacity and unemployment in most industries, businessmen and unions even in the defense sector might find it difficult to get price or wage increases. For a time, there could be an intermediate situation in which credit control brought marked recession and falling prices in one part of the economy while prices rose in the defense field. Beyond a certain point this imbalance would probably be redressed by the spread of inflation, although the spread of recession would be a possibility.

Indirect controls, however, can help prevent or halt a spiral. Tight credit and high business and personal income taxes can hold down demand and prevent or moderate price and wage increases that come from "demand pull." Significant examples are farm products and many food and clothing items the prices of which, not being "administered" by large firms, rise or fall quickly in response to changes in demand. Wages of unorganized labor often behave in the same way. To the extent to which increases in prices of cost-of-living items are choked off or moderated, one important element in the spiral will be slowed.

The Controls Needed to Curb a Spiral

A simplified but instructive view of the spiral reveals three interacting elements: (1) prices of basic materials going into munitions, capital goods and consumer durable goods; (2) prices of principal cost-of-living items—food, clothing, fuel and rent; and (3) wage rates. To prevent or halt a spiral each of these three must be controlled. The "package" of controls to do the job contains: (1) price ceilings on basic materials; (2) high personal income taxes plus price and rent ceilings to hold the cost of living; (3) wage ceilings—with tight credit and high business income taxes as general helpers.

Will the Spiral Start Again after Decontrol?

Suppose that a spiral has been stopped by these controls —will it start again whenever the price and wage controls are removed? The answer would be "No," were we in a business recession after a defense hump, with unemployment of several million and a generally poor business outlook. But the answer is not so easy if high prosperity and high employment continue after a defense build-up, whether defense spending flattens out or falls to a somewhat lower plateau.

Assume that a particular defense build-up, like that of the present, is over, but that large and steady defense spending is expected for many years ahead. Assume further that we have general prosperity and high employment, a balanced federal budget and controls that will keep credit from expanding faster than the physical volume of production (unless costs are raised by price and wage increases)—and an outlook that these conditions will continue. In this situation many prices will be at or close to their ceilings and some may be expected to go up if ceilings are removed.

In trying to answer the question, let us look at each of the three elements of the spiral.

The price ceilings on basic materials going into defense uses and into capital goods and consumer durable goods can be removed without substantial price increases if capacities have been expanded sufficiently and if business managements will administer these prices with one eye to general economic stability instead of charging all the traffic will bear. Thus in the postwar inflation of 1946-1948 and in the summer and fall of 1950 there were numerous instances of business companies holding "administered" prices below figures that could have been charged with existing demands. The price control agency could help to diminish the number of price increases after decontrol by seeing to it that toward the end of the period of price control ceiling prices included what were considered "normal" margins by "representative" firms.

Prices of most principal food and clothing items would remain fairly stable after decontrol if personal income taxes were high enough to eliminate an inflationary gap for consumer goods, and if food and clothing processors administered their margins with some regard for general economic stability.

In the field of fuels—coal, oil and wood—some prices are administered and some are determined largely by demand pull. What was said in the preceding paragraph applies to the fuel prices subject chiefly to demand pull; administered fuel prices call for the same treatment as do other administered prices.

This brings us to wages, which may present the most difficult problem of all. If large key unions demand and receive each year wage rate increases that exceed the annual average increase in man-hour productivity in the whole economy this would guarantee almost a perpetual spiral—under the conditions of high prosperity here assumed—because each year the average of unit labor costs in the economy would increase.

Reactions to Wage Demands, and Their Results

Some managements might try to resist the large wage demands. But in a period of high profits and tight manpower, many employers would settle more or less on labor's terms if the alternative were a strike or substantial loss of workers to other businesses. Some could pass on the higher labor costs in prices to customers, without much, if any, drop in sales volume. Examples are producers of defense products sold to the government, producers of necessities and sellers of commodities the demand for which was growing fast.

Even where a rise in price to cover the wage advance (or enough of it to permit profitable operation) did result in a substantial fall in sales volume it might still seem advisable to grant the wage increase—if the loss of sales volume from the price advance was estimated to be proportionately less than the loss of workers resulting from failure to meet the wage demand.

If many employers agree to large wage increases, many others will have to follow suit to hold their labor. A general round of wage increases raises labor incomes and thereby increases demand; this, in turn, tends to support higher prices.

It is hard to see how fiscal and credit controls alone could prevent large annual wage rate advances, unless these controls were drastic enough to bring about a marked recession and a change in the general business outlook in the nondefense part of the economy—a solution that would work only as long as we kept the recession.

The conclusion seems inescapable that in a period of high prosperity and favorable business outlook the labor unions have power to spark a perpetual spiral. Indeed, wage-induced price inflation might be more or less chronic in a continuous, full-employment peacetime economy, with only "normal" government expenditures. Many students of the problem of economic instability have come to regard this as one of our most serious peacetime problems.[16]

Conditions for Removal[17] of Price and Wage Controls

We seem to have come to this. We need general government price and wage controls to prevent or halt a spiral in a large defense build-up even in the absence of a general inflationary gap. Clearly, such controls can be removed if and when a drop in defense demand is accompanied by a general economic recession, or by a general subsidence of inflationary psychology even without a recession.

If inflationary attitudes do not disappear after defense demand flattens out or drops, most price and wage controls can still be removed with safety if (1) federal fiscal policy continues to prevent a general inflationary gap and credit expansion is held down to the rate of increase in physical volume of output; (2) capacities for most materials have been increased so there will be no shortages at stable prices; (3) most managements can be expected to "administer" prices with an eye to stability; (4) principal cost-of-living prices will be held stable by tax curbs on personal incomes and restraint by processors in holding to normal margins; and (5) most unions can be expected to hold their demands for general wage rate increases to no more than the pros-

16. See description of the present state of economists' thinking on this matter in a committee report, "The Problem of Economic Instability," by E. Despres, M. Friedman, A. G. Hart, P. Samuelson and D. H. Wallace, *American Economic Review,* September 1950, p. 535.

17. This section treats, in general, the problem of outright removal of price and wage controls. The issue of suspension versus removal is dealt with in Chapter 9.

pective average increase in man-hour productivity in the economy—probably about 2½ per cent a year. Unless these conditions are met, the spiral might start again after the removal of price and wage controls.

Managements administering prices with regard to general economic stability should try to hold down costs, thus forestalling the need for price increases. And prices should not be increased unless cost rises cut into normal profit margins.

If most unions and managements would restrict wage rate increases to figures in line with the average advance in productivity for the economy as a whole, wage-induced price inflation would not be a problem.[18] A good example is the provision in the contract between the United Automobile Workers of America-CIO and the General Motors Corporation giving an automatic annual increase of 4 cents an hour to all workers to let them share in the general rise in national productivity. The increase of 4 cents an hour represents a little over 2 per cent of the average hourly earnings of the auto workers. This provision is embodied in a five-year contract signed in May 1950. Thus it takes the place of annually bargained increases.[19]

Can We Count on Restraint by Business and Labor?

Restraint and statesmanship on the part of a number of

18. This is, of course, only a very general principle. Some particular labor groups, to say nothing of particular individuals, often are entitled, for one reason or another, to increases above the average for all.
Wage increases based on a prospective average increase in productivity for the economy would be inflationary if the actual average productivity increase should fall.

19. This provision was originally included in a two-year contract signed in May 1948. (The figure in that contract was 3 cents an hour.)
The present contract like the earlier one also provides for a quarterly adjustment in wage rates in step with changes in the consumers' price index of the Bureau of Labor Statistics. The question of policy toward such escalator clauses in periods of defense build-up is discussed in more detail in Chapter 10.

key unions and key corporations can probably do much to prevent an inflation spiral at times when there is no severe general inflationary pressure. However, this will not be easy for business and labor leaders. Stockholders and other businessmen may make it unpleasant for the business leader who wants to help stabilize prices. Labor leaders may find it hard to stay in elective office if they urge policies of moderation. There is no reason to be very optimistic about avoiding inflation if we have to depend heavily on voluntary restraint by business and labor. That is made plain enough by attitudes and actions in recent years.

But we ought to see clearly that during much or most of the defense period the alternatives to partial reliance on voluntary restraint by business and labor may be chronic inflation or continuous and effective direct price and wage controls—unless the defense program subsides to a low level, say less than 10 per cent of total national production, and stays there.

Direct Controls—Off and On

Suppose that after removal of general price and wage controls in 1953 a spiral of rising prices and wages occurs in the next two or three years in spite of tight fiscal and credit policies that prevent an inflationary gap. Should we restore direct controls? By 1956, this may be a $64 billion question.

This suggests another question: can we learn to turn off direct controls as soon as possible and turn them on again when they are needed? The discussion above indicates that this would be sensible in a defense period with a succession of humps and troughs of defense demand, or build-ups followed by plateaus of several years' duration.

This could probably be done with fair success for channeling controls on materials and accompanying price ceilings, and for shifting manpower and expanding plant capacities by various kinds of incentive controls. The case for these controls is fairly clear to most people and their interference with basic values and institutions is not great.

But when it comes to general price and wage controls, it is not easy to be optimistic. Again, however, we ought to see clearly what the alternatives are. They seem to be successive doses of inflation or continuous maintenance of price and wage controls—alternatives both of which would endanger our democratic values and institutions. That is the risk we face, unless we can learn to turn general wage and price controls on and off as needed.

Needed Statutory Provisions

The President should have continuous statutory authority to put on direct controls and take them off, in accordance with the needs of the situation. Congress does not usually move fast enough to pass a new law authorizing such controls at the moment they are required. On the other hand, the President might not remove general price and wage ceilings as soon as possible owing to pressures from the stabilization agencies and private groups who always "want to be sure" that all danger is over. Congress could remedy this, if necessary, by a joint resolution ending all existing ceilings except price ceilings linked to priority or allocation orders (see point (3) below) without rescinding the authority of the President to use general price and wage controls in another emergency.[20]

20. In a statement in June 1952, entitled *Ending Price-Wage Controls,* the Program Committee of the Committee for Economic Development registered its opposition to a policy of stand-by price and wage controls. This position seems to reflect: (1) a feeling that the authority to use such controls might

Congress should establish general standards to govern the use by the President of direct controls. Perhaps provisions something like the list below would be desirable. There are included here only the more general principles and the list is not exhaustive.

(1) Controls on use of materials and facilities may be used whenever these are required to make sure that defense needs are met fully and promptly. They should be removed whenever it seems clear that defense needs will be met fully and promptly without them.

(2) Expansion of capacity by business should be encouraged, in accordance with measures approved by Congress, wherever larger capacity will be needed to cover "regular" defense demands plus all other demands before controls on materials and facilities can be removed.

(3) A price ceiling may be established for any material under allocation or priority order. This should be removed when the allocation or priority order is lifted, unless it is needed as part of an existing program of general price and wage control.

---

be abused; and (2) a belief that in an inflationary emergency, Congress would quickly re-establish authority for price or wage controls by passing a joint resolution permitting a ninety-day general freeze of wages and prices. This author believes that Congress can go far to prevent abuse of the statutory authority for price and wage controls by laying down in the law appropriate standards and by establishing a joint watchdog committee with effective procedures. As the text suggests, we cannot be sure that Congress would re-establish controls quickly whenever they were needed. Furthermore, a ninety-day freeze would not last long enough to halt a price-wage spiral even if it were adequate to scotch a surge of panic buying. Prudence would call for the passage of an enabling law during the ninety-day period, giving stabilization powers and establishing standards for their use. Probably a better stabilization law can be passed in advance of an emergency than at a time when the pull and haul of pressures from interest groups have been increased by the existence of a general freeze of prices and wages.

(4) General price and wage controls may be established on declaration by the President of an inflationary emergency, arising from elements in the economic situation related to needed provision for defense, based on a finding that without these controls the average of wholesale prices will probably rise by 10 per cent or more within two years.

General price and wage controls should be removed on declaration by the President that the inflationary emergency is over, based on a finding that the average of wholesale prices will probably not increase, or at least not by more than 5 per cent, in the succeeding two years.

(5) The President should at all times use all existing powers, so far as practicable, to assist the direct controls in achieving their ends and to help create the conditions for their removal at the earliest possible date.

Direct and Indirect Controls Complementary

Direct and indirect controls are in the main complements rather than substitutes. It is sometimes argued that the weaker the indirect controls the stronger the need for direct controls and vice versa. For a short period, and within limits, there is some truth in this. But direct price and wage controls cannot long repress inflation in the face of continuous government deficit financing or too easy credit. On the other hand, indirect controls alone often cannot prevent a spiral of prices and wages, or a sudden buying surge, except by pushing us into recession. Indirect controls cannot break bottlenecks, but they can lessen their number. Channeling controls to deal with bottlenecks can be removed when capacities are increased sufficiently, provided indirect controls are adequate to curb general inflationary pressure.

5. Production Programming

"PRODUCTION PROGRAMMING" SOUNDS FORMIDABLE, and uninteresting. But we had better understand it—and demand it—because good production programming shows how to meet defense needs and at the same time get the largest possible output for civilians in the defense period. It also helps show when and where we need to apply controls on use of materials, facilities, manpower, prices and wages, and when these controls can be removed. In wartime production programming shows how to meet minimum civilian needs and at the same time get the largest possible output for military power.

Therefore, we want to know what production programming is and how it can be done effectively, although we can leave to the experts the technical details, which are often complex.

Programming—A Timetable for Production Goals

Production programming means determining feasible production goals on a timetable for planes, tanks, guns, shells, trucks, tires, railroad cars, army jackets, field ration units and other finished products; and for the aluminum, steel, copper, electronics, plastics, rubber, textiles and other materials going into them.

Production programming involves many things. First is the preparation of tentative production schedules or statements of requirements for munitions and other finished goods. These are then converted into requirements of materials and manpower. Next, estimates of supplies of the various materials and types of manpower are compared with the estimates of requirements. If these calculations show that available materials and manpower cannot fill all the requirements of military items, as originally stated, then some of the tentative production schedules must be cut back. Cutbacks are also in order if some items are out of line with others. There is no sense in making more airframes than engines to go in them, or more tank guns than will be needed to match the output of tanks plus extras for replacement.

In full war mobilization, everything that can add to military power will be in short supply. This means nearly all materials and nearly all kinds of manpower, because those not of direct military use can often be substituted in essential civilian goods or services for materials and manpower needed in military use. Thus, for example, wood can replace metals in furniture, railroad cars, temporary buildings and so on, and women can relieve men as bus drivers and messengers so that they can go into mines or other essential heavy work.

In wartime the requirements of military items as stated by the armed forces will always tend to be larger than can actually be produced with the available materials and manpower. Hence there will be a continuous job of making cutbacks to get production schedules that can be met, and production schedules that will give the best strategic balance of planes, tanks, guns and other munitions. Moreover, the military may try to cut production of civilian goods below the bedrock minimum necessary for efficiency in a maximum war effort.

Production Schedules in a "Readiness" Program

A "readiness" program calls for two sets of production schedules. One set is contingent: *if war breaks out* how many planes, tanks, guns and other munitions items are to be produced in the first year or two and on what timetable? If all goes well, government and industry will never have to use these schedules, but they must be laid out, at least roughly. If war *should* break out, and there were no such schedules in existence, precious months would be lost in the confusion of hurried, improvised programming.

The second set of schedules is the production guide for the defense program. With a limited defense take of only 15 to 25 per cent of the total national output, production programming might seem unnecessary. But even a limited defense program may at times require 50 to 75 per cent of the available supplies of some minerals, metals, chemicals, electronics or other materials or parts. The same may be true with respect to machine tool designers, tool and die makers, electronics engineers and other types of highly skilled manpower. Hence the need for a planned program for using these limited supplies of materials and manpower to achieve a balanced output of munitions for ourselves and our allies.

The job is complicated by the question of expanding facilities. How much of the scarce materials and manpower should be used for expansion at the expense of current production? In wartime, this becomes a very serious problem. In a readiness program, the extent of expansion should be related to the wartime set of schedules mentioned above. The same is true of stockpiles and "educational orders" required to make the wartime schedules realizable, should they be needed.

Production Schedules Are Procurement Schedules

"But," someone will ask, "isn't production programming just another term for the scheduling of procurement of munitions items and other things by the armed services, the Atomic Energy Commission and other government agencies"? The answer is "Yes," but calling it *production* programming points directly to the problems of feasibility of production. To flood the mills with procurement contracts reflecting impossibly high procurement schedules will only create a mess. For a time after Pearl Harbor, many procurement authorities of the armed services failed to realize that there were not enough materials and manpower to produce all they wanted of everything in the next year or two and that they would have to decide on the best feasible package of munitions. Once formulated, production schedules for the various items should become procurement schedules. Then procurement activities translate the total production schedule for tanks, or any other item, into individual company production schedules, as well as establishing contractual terms of purchase.

Given production and procurement schedules, it is the job of direct controls on materials, manpower and facilities to make actual output of each item correspond as closely as possible to scheduled output. In 1951-1953, as in World War II, much of the work of programming production of munitions has in fact been done in connection with the work of allocating aluminum, copper and steel, as will be explained later.

Current Programming of Munitions

This is the process of programming munitions for our defense effort in 1951-1952.

(1) Procurement sections of the Army, Navy and Air Force prepared production schedules in terms of physical units for 600 products representing about 75 per cent of the total dollar value of all military "hard goods," on a two-year timetable. These schedules reflected what the individual procurement sections considered the requirements in their fields of responsibility.

(2) Each procurement section next broke down these end-product schedules into requirements of materials by months and by quarters.[1] For the three basic materials—aluminum, copper and steel—these requirement schedules of the various sections of the armed forces showed, at any given time monthly requirements for the first six months, quarterly requirements for the next twelve months, and lump-sum, six-month requirements for the following half year. Programming of requirements for a number of other important metals, such as tin, lead, zinc, cobalt, tungsten and nickel, was done on a quarterly basis.

(3) The next step was transmission of these proposed production schedules for end items and materials to the Munitions Board, an organization composed of a civilian chairman and the undersecretaries of the Army, Navy and Air Force. The Munitions Board was responsible for coordinating the procurement and production plans of the three armed

1. In this job it is necessary to make allowance for "pipeline" requirements—the amounts of materials that have to go into working inventories of raw materials and parts and subassemblies at every stage in the production of finished planes, guns or ammunition. Allowance also must be made for the length of time between the receipt of a material or parts and the completion of the finished product—a kind of "lead time." The phrase "lead time" is used in other connections. For example, it refers to the length of time between placing a contract and delivery of the product. For new aircraft this "lead time" seems currently to average eighteen to twenty-four months. With new models of a product this "lead time" will usually exceed that for materials because of time needed for tooling up, trial runs and other preparations for production.

forces. In the Munitions Board these proposed programs were reviewed by divisions corresponding to major programs —that is, the aircraft program, the ship program, the electronics program, the weapons and ammunition program, and the like. The purpose of processing all individual schedules in the Munitions Board was to develop an integrated program for the Department of Defense as a whole. This involved a lot of balancing, trimming and readjustment.

(4) The integrated program of the Defense Department was sent to the requirements section of the Defense Production Administration, the agency charged with the over-all programming responsibility. Here the schedules from the Defense Department met the schedules from the Atomic Energy Commission, the Maritime Administration and the other so-called "claimant" agencies—agencies that draw up requirements of materials and submit them to DPA as claims.

(5) The Defense Production Administration assembled estimates of available supplies of materials and parts and facilities for defense production, and compared them with the requirements submitted by claimant agencies.

(6) The Requirements Committee of DPA then decided how the materials were to be divided up for the next quarter among the programs proposed by the claimant agencies.[2] This tested the realism or feasibility of the proposed production schedules. If there were not enough materials to carry them all out simultaneously, the Requirements Committee had to decide which programs were to be cut back, and by how much. This central review also weeded out instances of imbalance in stated requirements that would involve

2. "Next" quarter here means the next quarter to be programmed. In practice, program determinations must be made several months ahead. That is, work on third-quarter programs is being done in the first quarter.

accumulating parts or end items before they could actually be used, because complementary parts or end items were not there.

If, as a result of all this, the Defense Department or any other claimant found that it had been allotted less of any materials than its proposed programs called for, it had to review its production schedules and decide where to trim them. After this set of decisions it could firm up production schedules for the next quarter for the items in its purview and arrange for its contractors to get the necessary materials.[3]

Civilian Production Also Must Be Programmed

So far, we have been talking about programming military production. But many civilian products use the same kinds of materials and manpower—e.g., commercial planes, automobiles, trucks, radios, television sets, refrigerators, locomotives, railroad cars, houses, schools, stores, churches, theatres and race tracks. In full war when all civilian consumption must be held down to bedrock minimum, production of essential civilian goods and services must be programmed almost as carefully as military goods. The armed forces are not, of course, the best judges of minimum civilian needs. These estimates must be made by a civilian agency. For the less essential civilian goods and services—housewares, book paper, movies, baseball, for example—it can be a broadbrush operation.

3. This brief and simplified description of production programming and allocation of key materials might imply that the procurement sections of the armed forces wait to place procurement contracts until their production programs have been ratified by allotments of scarce materials. This, of course, is not the way it happens. In practice, the procurement sections place contracts for substantial amounts of munitions before the programming job is completed. But the timing of deliveries on these contracts and the amounts of products obtained on additional contracts have to fit the approved production schedules and corresponding allotments of materials.

In a limited defense program civilian production does not need to be programmed or controlled in the same high degree. But the program authorities must make estimates of the unrestricted output of the various civilian goods in order to see where shortages are severe enough to require direct controls. In most areas military requirements alone would not outrun available supplies of materials and manpower, but in many cases military production plus unrestricted civilian consumption would do so. Specific shortages must be identified so that prompt plans to deal with them can be made. In these instances the Requirements Committee of DPA must include provision for civilian uses in dividing up the available materials (the process described in point (6) in the last section). If filling all the military requests would leave a serious shortage in certain vital civilian goods the military may have to be cut back somewhat.

Where the needs of the armed forces can be filled without creating civilian shortage, programming of civilian production is not necessary. In 1951 and 1952 this was the case in most food products, apparel and other soft goods.

Thus the scope of production programming depends directly on the size of the defense or war program. In full war, production programming, like everything else, must be "all out." In a limited defense program it must be substantial, but can be far short of "across the board."

Production Schedules and Manpower

Although production programming is operated in connection with allocations of basic materials, production schedules all along the line should also reflect the manpower situation, present and prospective. This was not well done in World War II. The defect did not have serious consequences only because there were few acute manpower shortages until we were beyond the peak of production needs.

For the present defense program the Bureau of Labor Statistics has adequate data on the labor force with breakdowns by area, occupational classifications, age, sex, etc. Current unemployment figures have been satisfactory, but statistics of manpower requirements have been inadequate. Field offices of the U.S. Bureau of Employment Security obtained estimates from industry for several months ahead. These forecasts by industry substantially reflected defense contracts already let. Thus, in part, the manpower requirements of a defense production program are not known until the contracts are placed and the program is under way!

In World War II the armed forces and the war agencies developed statistical techniques of estimating requirements of parts and materials for many end items, through the use of conversion factors. The number of pounds of aluminum, the amount of copper, ferroalloys, plastics, rubber and other materials going into a B-17 were figured out. Once these conversion factors were determined, it was a relatively speedy matter to compute the requirements of each material for any given number of "Flying Fortresses." With conversion factors for all the important munitions items, statisticians could estimate for basic materials the approximate requirements of a munitions program whatever its scale. To be sure, the armed forces have not determined conversion factors for all important munitions or all basic materials.

Presumably the same process can be applied to the various types of manpower. The Bureau of Labor Statistics and the Air Force have been working on a promising scheme, often referred to as "input-output analysis," whereby any bill of goods can be translated by use of standard factors into requirements of manpower as well as materials.[4] Meanwhile efforts are being continued to improve current reporting of industry projections of manpower needs and estimates of changes in the manpower situation, area by area.

Results of Production Programming

The need for production programming becomes clear if we look at the results, both for military objectives and for the civilian economy.

In the first place, programming permits feasible production schedules which express military strategy in terms of the volume and assortment of weapons and other equipment. Furthermore, programming shows where the total of stated requirements cannot be met with available materials, facilities and manpower, and hence where individual schedules must be trimmed, so that they can all be carried out. Instances in which production takes longer than estimated also come to light and call for schedule readjustments, as in the case of aircraft in the second half of 1951.

Programming also shows military authorities the relative costs, in terms of materials and manpower, of different kinds of weapons and military equipment. Air Force generals can then compare the relative economic cost of various fighter planes with their relative military performance. This helps put the aluminum, copper and manpower-hours into the planes that will give the best military results per unit of materials and manpower used. Similar calculations can help decide whether to have more bombers and fewer fighters,

4. Techniques for this type of analysis, which also has application to problems of peacetime, were first developed by Professor Wassily Leontief of the Department of Economics of Harvard University. See Wassily W. Leontief, *The Structure of the American Economy, 1919-1939*, Oxford, New York, 1951.

more tanks and less artillery, or more air wings and fewer ships or army divisions.

Production programming makes it possible to compare the relative economic costs of military and civilian programs in the same terms. It should give both military and civilian officials a better understanding of actual needs in both fields, and of the effects on civilian production of enlarging the military program, and vice versa. Production programming does not, however, provide any precise quantitative comparison of the relative benefits to be obtained from more military production as against more civilian production.

Elimination of Waste

Second, good programming cuts out two kinds of waste: the waste of trying to get more than is possible of everything; the waste of unbalanced output of the various parts and materials of an end item.

Without feasible production schedules wartime procurement agencies would try to get more of most munitions than could be produced with available materials and manpower. With all sights set too high the scarcer materials and parts would bottleneck production of most items, while other parts and subassemblies of the same items piled up in unusable inventories. Precious materials and manpower would be used to expand facilities for aircraft and tank assembly plants that could not be fully operated for lack of aluminum or special alloy steels. Individual procurement sections and their prime contractors would try to buy up materials and components far ahead of need, to make sure of fulfilling *their* responsibilities.

Without good programming, parts, subassemblies and basic materials would be produced in haphazard, unbalanced quantities. This would mean a continuous succession of crises with production authorities trying feverishly to relieve one desperate shortage after another. For example, just as a bottleneck of fractional horsepower motors was broken, deliveries of generators would fall off, owing to a shortage of wiring, caused by an extreme scarcity of copper. And so on and on.

The most effective prosecution of war requires elimination of these wastes. Only good production programming makes that possible. In wartime, with civilian consumption at bedrock minimum, these wastes would reduce war production.

In a limited defense program such wastes probably would not be allowed to cut defense production. Imbalances would take the form of more or less continuous excess production and idle stocks of various materials and parts of defense goods. Hence, in a limited defense program these wastes would probably reduce civilian production.

Current Production as against Expanding Capacity

Third, good production programming will aid greatly in determining which industries should have increased capacity, and the relative amount of increase. In full war mobilization, programming will show where production falls short of meeting minimum needs. Equally important, it will highlight the difficult question: is it wiser to use a given amount of scarce materials or manpower for current production of war goods or to expand future capacity to produce more war goods or their parts and materials?

In a readiness program it is important to expand plant capacity for munitions, and plant and equipment for materials. Without a programming operation, determinations of capacity expansion would be hit-or-miss. After the initial wave of industrial expansions needed primarily on security grounds, further capacity increases may be desirable, as explained in the last chapter, to meet civilian demands and make it possible to lift channeling controls and other restrictions as soon as possible. Good production programming will help determine the relative amounts of expansion needed in various industries for this purpose.

Finally, statistics on supplies and requirements developed in the programming operation will help determine when and where there must be direct controls on use of resources, on prices and on wages. Similarly, they will aid in deciding when controls may be removed.

Production Programming Is a Continuous Process

Production programming, as here described, sounds fairly simple. That is because the account was made easy to follow. But this is not to imply that there are no difficulties. In practice production programming is a very complex job. Determining the validity of many—and often conflicting—stated requirements, estimating available supplies, designing an accounting system and administrative procedures to keep track of actual production and of the use of materials and manpower, and eliminating loopholes—these and other problems present countless difficulties.

Another misconception is that production programming is a one-shot affair, that all the production schedules are tested, firmed up, signed and sealed at the same time, to remain static for several years. At any given time the military may not have determined how many it wants of some weapons, or Congress may not have acted on appropriations.

For example, late in 1951 it seemed probable that the goal of the Air Force would be raised well above the 95 air wings set in 1950, but the exact figure had not been fixed. Furthermore, when we are not actually at war on a large scale it is possible to hold down the stock of particular planes, tanks, guns or guided missiles if more promising types are on the drawing boards. This is another way of saying that a change from one weapon to another, from one plane model to another, will require a change in many production schedules including the affected parts, subassemblies and materials. The same is true, of course, for substantial design changes. We do not want to freeze production schedules of munitions, except when actual or imminent war calls for immediate quantity production of the best models then possessed.

Production schedules must be revised continuously in the light of experience. If production of jet engines takes more time than was contemplated their schedule must be revised and with it the schedule for airframes.

There are also other reasons why there never is a complete production program at any given time—for example, lack of adequate statistics in some fields. The program can never be a neat blueprint. But despite all the difficulties, complexities and changes, if production programming is well done it can help enormously to get the utmost out of materials, facilities and manpower in terms of military power and civilian living standards.

6. Controls on Use of Materials

WHEN MATERIALS AND MANPOWER are insufficient to meet goals for military production, defense-supporting production and unrestricted civilian demands, direct controls will be needed.

In the present defense program, as in World War II, chief reliance for getting the right "pattern" of production has been placed on controls over the key materials, especially aluminum, steel and copper—the materials that enter most extensively into military hard goods, transportation equipment, power plants, building construction and other defense-supporting activities. The allocation scheme used for these three metals is the Controlled Materials Plan, or CMP.

Controls over materials can limit effectively their use outside the area of defense and defense-supporting activities, and channel them into military items and other needed products in accordance with the schedules of the production program. These controls will make it possible to get along most of the time, at least, without government orders to men and women to move from one job to another. Where civilian output has to be cut back for lack of materials, layoffs will usually make more manpower available for the expanding defense production. Then a combination of appeals, training programs and various incentives can usually attract sufficient labor into most defense work and solve all but acute manpower shortages.[1]

Why Control Materials Rather Than Manpower?

On paper, it would be possible to get the same results in

1. The next chapter explains and elaborates this point.

production control by allocating key types of labor as by controlling the use of basic materials. But ordering workers from one job to another is a much greater infringement of human freedom than ordering materials to change jobs. Of course, allocation of materials restricts the freedom of business managers to sell wherever they wish, but it does not order *them* to move from one location to another or to take a different kind of job. This is sufficient reason for putting compulsory controls on materials instead of on manpower.

It is worth noting in addition that to work out an equitable scheme to allocate manpower would be much harder than to design an equitable allocation for materials. Aluminum ingots do not have differences in seniority rights, or in the number of dependents, or in schooling and housing needs.

Allocation of materials may cause unemployment in some areas or firms and the workers affected may have to move occupationally or geographically to get other jobs. This may reflect merely the necessities of the defense program, or it may be the result of mistakes on the part of allocation authorities—often it is not easy to tell which. In some instances, unemployment and job change will be minor in extent because firms can substitute other materials in civilian production or take on additional defense production.

Three Questions about Materials Controls

There are three principal questions about controls on materials: What kinds of materials controls are needed in full war? What materials situation have we faced in the present defense program and what kinds of materials controls are appropriate for this or for similar future build-ups? When direct materials controls are needed at times during the defense period can we apply types of controls and policies that will not impair the strength and vigor of our free economy?

Materials Controls in Full War

Full war would require use of virtually the full battery of controls affecting supplies and use of materials: production limitation and simplification orders, conservation orders, allocation schemes, inventory restrictions, measures to increase domestic production and imports, preclusive buying abroad and other methods of economic warfare.

Production limitation orders prohibit all production of specified articles or limit the volume of permitted production. The purpose is to encourage conversion of plant to war production and to free materials and manpower for war uses. In World War II output of passenger automobiles and other consumer durable goods was prohibited. Production of trucks and some other essential civilian goods was limited to specified quantities per quarter.

Simplification orders also conserve materials and manpower by cutting out "trim," gadgets and more expensive models. Work-a-day models of trucks, stoves, hot-water heaters, farm equipment and other essential items can be made with saving of materials and manpower—especially when production is standardized to a few sizes and styles on which plants can make long runs. Simplification also can bring savings of materials and manpower in soft goods. Women's dresses can be designed for a slim, short silhouette. Manufacture of men's vests and double-breasted suits can be prohibited.

Conservation orders are intended to husband short materials. They prohibit or limit use of materials in a specified list of products.[2] In World War II, conservation orders banned many uses of copper, aluminum, zinc, rubber, nickel and many other materials.

In a future all-out war extensive use of conservation orders would probably be an indication of partial failure in mobilizing the economy. Conservation orders permit maintenance of output if managements can find substitute materials. This may create shortages of these substitute materials. And, even more important, it retains manpower in civilian output and puts a drag on conversion of civilian plants to war production. In full-war production, limitation and simplification orders are needed. Conservation orders should not be used then except as stop-gap measures or in situations, if any, where production limitation orders or allocation programs are impracticable because of great administrative difficulties, lack of personnel to operate them or intractable political opposition.

Production limitation orders and conservation orders can greatly reduce the demand for particular materials. But they may not free just the right amounts of materials needed for war production. Obviously, such orders cannot ensure the flow of materials and parts to the various war uses and users in the balanced proportions required by production schedules. Hence precise channeling controls are also needed.

Priorities, sometimes called preference ratings, are a rudimentary form of channeling control. Normal business practice is to fill orders on a "first-come-first-served" basis. If war orders came when companies had heavy backlogs of other

2. Excise taxes on scarce materials would tend to have the same effect. See Albert G. Hart and E. Cary Brown, *Financing Defense,* p. 51. It would be very difficult, however, to predict the amount of reduction in use of a material from a given amount of tax, or to vary the tax as often as changes in the amount of conservation were needed.

orders, the war orders would not be filled for a long time unless they were pushed up ahead on the list. Priority certificates, issued by procurement sections or other defense authorities, are intended to do this and also to show the relative urgency of need for various munitions items and other essential goods. Relative urgency is indicated by ratings or symbols such as A-1, A-2, A-3, . . . B-1, B-2, B-3, . . . and so on.

Priorities can also be used to indicate the relative urgency of different uses of materials and parts, when makers of end products "extend" their end-product ratings (A-1, A-4, or B-2 as the case may be) to their suppliers on orders for materials or parts. But in "extending" to suppliers his priority rating for airplane engines a manufacturer can put down just about any estimates his conscience will allow for the supply of parts and materials he will require.

If he wants to build up a reserve stock of materials and parts so he will not be caught short on future contracts, or to get some materials for civilian business, who will know? Thus there can be no strict quantitative control of the flow of materials and parts by priorities alone. Furthermore, priority certificates are seldom issued for a specified period, say for the first quarter of the year, to expire at the end of that three-month period. They are good until they are used, so no one ever knows the total priority claims on steel sheets in a given quarter. The sheet maker knows the volume of priorities he has received but he does not know how many more will come in today or tomorrow.

Priorities can be useful in moderate shortages, such as those in 1940 and 1950, but they soon become ineffectual as the shortages become severe. This is because more and more priority paper is issued, and new ratings such as AA-1 and AAA have to be invented to ensure early delivery. In 1941, there was a flood of priority paper and new, higher ratings were introduced. In 1942 the inflation of priorities became so acute that the system broke down.

The Complete Allocation of Wartime

In full war there is little use for priorities. There must be complete *allocation* of almost all important materials and parts—both of war goods and of essential civilian goods. Complete allocation of a material means that the whole available supply for a given period, say the first quarter of the year, is divided between uses and users by a system of allotments. Specific amounts are allotted to designated users for specified purposes.

Allocation means strict quantitative control. Almost every ton of steel or pound of copper can be accounted for.[3] If a user does not consume his allotment in one quarter, that will show up in the inventory figures he must report (assuming he reports correctly). Prohibition of inventories of materials and parts that are larger than needed for working inventories is, of course, essential to an allocation program. If a firm's inventory goes above the allowable figure the excess would be figured as part of its allotment for a later period, received in advance.

But to have allocation programs for all the important materials and parts is not, in itself, enough. They must be keyed together so that allocations of the various materials to each producer are *balanced*. Allotments of steel, columbium, copper and other materials to makers of parts for jet engines must fit so that the makers of parts can operate efficiently—

3. We have to say "almost" because in practice it is not worthwhile to do all the extra work that would be required to account completely for all deliveries by small, obscure sellers of a material.

and so that engine makers will not be held up by imbalance in the flow of parts to them.

In World War II, the Controlled Materials Plan represented the development of an integrated control system. This was a complete and detailed allocation scheme for steel, copper, aluminum and their alloys. Allocations of many other materials were indirectly affected by provisions that keyed them to the allotments of these three basic materials. Should there be another total war the CMP type of control would probably need to be extended to other materials or other types of effective allocation scheme developed.[4]

Existence of comprehensive and detailed allocation programs for the basic materials most extensively used in war goods and war-supporting activities would mean, however, that allocation of a number of subsidiary materials probably could be made to "follow along" by roughly keying their control into the basic allocation programs, without setting up a detailed system for each of these secondary materials.

In a future war there would also have to be a much closer link between allocation controls on materials and manpower controls than existed in World War II. This was not a serious problem then because, as noted before, there were few severe manpower shortages—a fact that reflected both the severe unemployment at the start of the defense program (8 million in 1940) and the great increase in the number of women workers and older and younger people going into war work.

4. To be effective an allocation scheme must be designed to fit the structure of the market for the material to be allotted and to make use of existing business practices as far as possible. Hence, although the job to be done is the same in all allocation schemes, their basic principles, as well as details, have to be somewhat different. Design of allocation schemes is a highly technical and complex matter that must be left out of this book. For conclusions and suggestions on extension of the CMP type of allocation and development of

Price ceilings, of course, can help make allocations work. Unless prices are stabilized there will be strong inducements to hoard materials, thus violating allocation regulations, and to look for extra large profit margins. This will be true of the prudent, who want insurance against inflation, as well as of the greedy.

The Materials Situation in 1951-1952

The readiness program launched in 1950 calls for supplies of strategic and critical materials large enough for four things: (1) to equip the enlarged armed forces (here and abroad) established by the defense program; (2) to provide ample munitions for the armed forces operating in Korea; (3) to provide materials for a substantial expansion of plant capacity for munitions, power and the basic materials themselves; and (4) to build stockpiles of materials adequate to support the output of munitions needed for a considerable initial period of full war, if that should come.

This means exceptionally large demands for most materials. For example, in May 1951 the NPA Administrator estimated that imminent demands for certain basic metals would be about 140 per cent of available supplies.[5] In June 1951 the same official said the demand for steel was 35 per cent above supply, and in August of that year the steel demand for the final quarter, his figures showed, would be almost 50 per cent larger than available supply.[6]

---

others, see Edwin B. George and Robert Landry, "Controlling Resource Flows in Wartime," *American Economic Review*, June 1950, p. 323.

5. Address by Manly Fleischmann, NPA Administrator, at meeting of Defense Advisory Committee, Department of the Interior, May 9, 1951, p. 5 (mimeographed).

6. Manly Fleischmann, NPA Administrator, Press Conference, June 13, 1951, p. 10 (mimeographed), and Radio Speech, August 7, 1951.

In August, the fourth-quarter aluminum demand appeared to be more than 140 per cent of available supply; for copper wire the figure was above 150 per cent; and for structural steel, over 200 per cent.[7]

Defense Production Administration estimates of requirements or "demand" stated by claimant agencies for the first quarter of 1952 showed needs above resources for seven key materials ranging from 156 per cent of available supply for carbon steel to 189 per cent for copper foundry products. (See Table 5.)

TABLE 5

ESTIMATED EXCESS OF DEMAND OVER SUPPLY,
FIRST QUARTER, 1952

Material	Stated Requirements as Percentage of Available Supply
Carbon steel	156
Alloy steel	159
Stainless steel	168
Brass mill copper products	175
Wire mill copper products	166
Foundry copper products	189
Aluminum	177

Source: Defense Production Administration, Office of Program and Requirements, *Background for Program Determinations and Allocations of Steel, Copper and Aluminum for the First Quarter, 1952,* p. 4 (November 2, 1951).

The preceding estimates of excess of demand over supply may be exaggerated because they are based on stated requirements from claimant agencies. Such "requirements" often contain some "water" to allow for expected cutbacks. Even

7. All the fourth-quarter estimates are from the second source cited in the preceding footnote.

so they indicate substantial shortages. Moreover, some parts of unrestricted demand are not registered where conservation orders have prohibited or limited certain uses of the materials.

During 1952, shortages diminished for many materials as a result of higher domestic production, larger imports, or a decline in military or civilian demand. In the second quarter of the year, controls on materials were revoked in twenty and relaxed in twenty-six instances.[8] However, the prolonged steel stoppage in the middle of the year forced postponement of scheduled liberalization of the regulation of the use of steel; and in many other instances shortages were still substantial.

For most of the important materials, the defense program calls for expansion of capacity to produce the material, or accumulation of a stockpile or both. The second is more important where we are dependent in large degree on imports —for example, cobalt, manganese and tin. In such materials as steel, aluminum and many chemicals where domestic production can carry most of the load, expansion of capacity has a high priority in the present defense program, as explained in Chapter 4.

Free World Supplies

This country depends on foreign sources for a number of basic materials. We import very little lumber or sulphur. But in substantial quantities we rely on other countries for a number of key commodities, for example, cobalt, lead, manganese ore, tin, tungsten, wool, and rubber. (See Table 6.)

8. *Sixth Quarterly Report of the Director of Defense Mobilization,* July 1, 1952, p. 25.

TABLE 6

UNITED STATES CONSUMPTION AND PRODUCTION OF
SELECTED COMMODITIES AS PERCENTAGE OF
FREE WORLD PRODUCTION, 1950

Commodity	Consumption[a]	Production
Items not largely imported:		
Lumber	72	66
Sulphur:		
Native	66	93
All forms	43	56
Items imported in substantial quantities:		
Aluminum	63	51
Cobalt[b]	63	4
Copper[b]	61	38
Iron ore	54	51
Lead[b]	64	29
Manganese ore	56	4
Nickel[b]	68	..
Petroleum	62	57
Rubber (natural and synthetic)	53	20
Tin[b]	65	..
Tungsten[b]	65	23
Wood pulp (mechanical and chemical)	52	43
Wool	32	6
Zinc[b]	55	33

Source: Council of Economic Advisers, *The Economic Situation at Mid-year, 1951*, p. 74, Table 3. (The figures were compiled by the Department of State.)

a. Apparent consumption (production plus imports minus exports), except for rubber and wool for which estimates of actual consumption are used. Additions to domestic stocks are included in apparent consumption.

b. Production represents metal content of mine production.

Other nations, including our allies in the North Atlantic Treaty Organization, are in the same boat with respect to many of these materials, including copper, tin, tungsten and wool. Most of the materials important to us are of equal importance for their defense programs. Clearly, the free nations should band together to secure large amounts of these materials and also to adopt measures to prevent competition among themselves from producing an allocation that is unfair or inconsistent with an integrated joint defense program.[9]

With these ends as well as price stabilization in view, an International Materials Conference of major producing and consuming countries began meetings in Washington early in 1951. Fourteen commodities have been under study by the Conference. Commodity committees of the Conference recommended patterns of distribution for tungsten, molybdenum, sulphur, copper, nickel, cobalt and zinc—all of which except zinc were still considered necessary in mid-1952. In most cases the recommendations registered unanimous agreement on allocations, even though acceptance was voluntary. It is said that this work of the IMC slowed extravagant bidding for scarce materials and helped check the price increases that began in 1950.[10]

In some cases, stabilization may call for reduction or suspension of import duties or use of subsidies to buy at the world price and resell to domestic users at a lower price. Where the imported material goes largely or entirely into end items purchased by the government, this is not a subsidy in the ordinary sense. In fact, the government saves money by such "subsidies" wherever they avoid either a price rise on that portion of the supply of a material produced at home or a pyramiding of a price increase on imported materials in the prices of end items.

Materials Controls Needed for a Defense Build-up

In a sharp defense build-up such as that of 1950-1953

9. In the last analysis this gets down to an agreement on relative quantities of materials that each country is to get for its own civilian production—including production for export, which is important to countries with a "dollar shortage" or other balance of payments problems.

10. *Fifth Quarterly Report of the Director of Defense Mobilization,* April 1, 1952, p. 26.

marked shortages of a number of materials will be unavoidable even with the best that can be done to enlarge imports and domestic supplies. Channeling controls of some kind will be necessary, at least temporarily.

In the early stage of a defense program, before the defense take of materials becomes a large proportion of supplies, a combination of conservation orders, prohibiting or limiting nonessential uses, and priorities and inventory control will probably be sufficient to assure adequate supplies of materials to defense production and supporting activities.[11]

This was the policy of the National Production Authority in 1950 and the first half of 1951. Conservation orders restricted the nondefense use of copper, aluminum, zinc and a number of other materials, chiefly metals. For April-June 1951, nondefense users of copper were limited to 75 per cent of average use in the first half of 1950. For the same quarter, the permitted use of aluminum was 65 per cent of that in the same base period. Some nonessential uses of these and other metals in short supply were prohibited.

Priorities were used in 1950 and 1951 but the authorities, mindful of the lessons of a decade ago, were careful to limit their issuance. In contrast to the A, B and C ratings of 1941 —to say nothing of the AA and AAA ratings feverishly introduced as shortages became more acute—only a single band rating, called a DO (defense order) rating, was used this time. In other words, there were no degrees of preference among rated orders. Procurement sections assigned DO ratings to their contracts. Their contractors "extended" the DO rating to their suppliers of parts or materials.

When materials shortages become marked the combina-

11. This statement would hold even if demand for materials to rebuild government stockpiles was quite large, provided the conservation orders were made drastic enough.

tion of conservation orders and priorities will not ensure a flow of materials and parts to all producers of military and defense-supporting production in the right pattern to fit the production schedules. Allocation then becomes necessary.

When Material Allocation Is Needed

There is no magic figure of the excess of demand over supply to tell exactly when an allocation scheme should be established for a material. If the excess demand is less than, say, 15 per cent, allocation probably will not be necessary. If it is more than 35 per cent, allocation probably will be needed.

But there are also other considerations. One is the number of individual instances in which producers of munitions and other required articles are having difficulty in getting adequate supplies of the material, even with priorities. Another is the prevailing psychology. If everyone expects the shortage of a material to become more acute, or the price of the material to rise sharply, allocation may be needed sooner than indicated by statistical estimates of the excess of physical volume of demand over the supply.

Much depends also on how long a substantial excess of demand over supply is likely to last. If it appears to be a matter of a year or two, an allocation scheme surely will be needed, and there is much to be said for establishing it a little early, so as to get it working well when the pinch becomes tight.

There are several reasons why allocation should replace priority control when shortage becomes marked.

1. If the allocation is well done, it is the most effective way of directing materials and parts in the right proportions

to defense users. Hence, it makes for maximum efficiency in defense production.

2. When allocation keeps down imbalances in the flow of materials it makes larger supplies available for civilian uses.

3. Allocation can help make larger supplies available for civilian use by forcing a tighter programming of requirements. An allocation scheme enables a central review of all proposed production schedules before materials are allotted. This can pare down overstatements of materials requirements without lowering the output of defense goods. Allocation can also prevent or minimize the natural tendency of procurement sections and their contractors and suppliers to buy ahead of needs. Overbuying becomes more difficult with a system that makes allotments only to cover requirements of the ensuing month, quarter or half year.

Steel, Copper, Aluminum and Other Metals

In mid-1951, the Controlled Materials Plan was established to allocate steel, copper and aluminum, much as was done in World War II. In large degree the use of these metals in consumer durable goods and nondefense construction had to be cut back. A complete allocation system seemed to promise fairer treatment of all business enterprises in these fields than a scramble for the very limited supplies left over after allocations for defense needs including construction and expansion of defense equipment.

Nickel, molybdenum, cobalt, columbium and tungsten were brought under allocation early in the defense program. Allocation schemes for cadmium, lead, tin, zinc and several chemicals were set up later.[12]

12. It should not be inferred from the above that the author has made a finding, one way or another, with respect to the necessity of any of these particular allocation programs. It is not the purpose of this study to make de-

Limitation Orders in a Defense Period

We noted earlier that production limitation orders are needed in a full war program to encourage conversion of facilities from civilian to war use and to free both labor and materials for war production. It does not appear, however, that production limitation orders are needed in a defense program like the present one.[13]

With the aim of adding greatly to defense plant capacity, no large conversion of facilities from civilian to defense use has been desired. The manpower situation has not become serious enough to justify production limitation orders for the purpose of freeing manpower for defense use. Materials shortages have been cared for by a combination of conservation orders, priorities and allocations.

Does a defense program like the present require orders that eliminate trim, gadgets and the like or orders cutting out or limiting production of more expensive models of a product—more expensive in terms of materials and manpower as well as price?

Orders of this kind are not necessary to ensure that defense needs are met. So long as there is enough of the material available to cover defense needs allocation can direct the required amount to defense. The question is whether or not orders of this kind are needed to enlarge the number of items for civilian use.

It is not easy to develop standards for this problem. If the quantity of a material saved by cutting out trim and the like

---

tailed surveys and appraisals of the various aspects of the current defense program.

13. Orders specifying authorized production in units have been issued only for a few things—e.g., railroad equipment and motor vehicles. In both these cases ceilings in units seem to have been set somewhat above the amounts that materials allotments could produce without conservation, substitution or changes of other sorts.

will keep in production some civilian articles that would otherwise have to be banned, most of us would probably favor a simplification order. The same can be said of material savings sufficient to keep in business efficient producers who otherwise would have to shut down for lack of a material for which no satisfactory substitute was obtainable.

If the output of cars were slated to drop below, say, 50 per cent of predefense production for two or three years it would probably be desirable to cut out or severely restrict the output of higher-priced cars that use more materials per car, in the interest of turning out a larger number of units. Perhaps many would favor this if car production were to fall only to 70 per cent. But with the large stocks of relatively new cars in the hands of consumers in recent years essential needs seem unlikely to suffer unless car output is cut much more than this. The same seems true for most other consumer durable goods—refrigerators, automatic washers, power mowers and so on.

Policies to Help Keep a Strong Free Economy

In full war every citizen must for the time being become, in effect, a member of the government. Normal civilian life has to be put in mothballs "for the duration." Only those civilian needs the satisfaction of which is necessary to the war effort can be permitted to use economic resources. The job is clear-cut and everyone has to do his part. In the limited programs of a long defense period our task, in a way, is more difficult. Many restrictions will have to be applied if we are serious in the defense effort, and we must be sure that we are using the controls necessary to the job. At the same time, we must preserve a strong, free civilian economy so far as consistent with meeting defense needs. The extent and kind of direct controls and the policies used in their administration must be decided with both these ends in view.

Let us look now at the question of keeping the civilian economy as free and strong as possible. The solution of this problem involves several factors: (1) removal of controls as soon as considerations of defense permit; (2) holding the defense take of materials down to the amount actually needed; (3) avoiding, as far as possible, orders or policies that force businesses to shut down, keep new businesses from starting up, or prevent the introduction of new products or varieties of products; (4) allowing the satisfaction of the broadest possible range of freely expressed consumer demands.

Rapid expansion of materials capacities to permit early removal of controls was emphasized in Chapter 4. In succeeding pages we have noted the advantages of tight programming and effective, "keyed-together" channeling controls in saving materials for civilian uses.

Orders that limit production force plants to shut down or curtail output. Conservation orders and allocations of materials do not have this result where substitute materials can be used. Hence these techniques are more in line with the aim of keeping all parts of the civilian economy as healthy as possible and filling the broadest possible range of consumer demands. Production limitation orders can and should be confined to cases where it is essential to convert to military production all or a large part of the facilities of a particular industry—cases that are likely to be as rare in a limited defense program as they will be numerous in full war.[14]

14. It is conceivable that a production limitation order might be the only way to convert to military production a particular group of workmen with

Principles for Distribution of Materials

While materials controls are in effect, what principles should determine the distribution of materials going into civilian use? One easy answer is that after 100 per cent provision for military products, all regular users of a material should receive an equal percentage of their consumption of the material in an appropriate base period. For example, each fabricator of aluminum would be permitted to use in nonmilitary production 55 per cent of his use of aluminum in civilian products in a predefense period. This answer is too simple but it underlines a sound principle: equality among firms in sharing materials available after defense needs have been met.

However, allocations for defense must extend far beyond military goods. Railroad cars and locomotives, electric power, housing and hospital equipment for new military installations and defense plants, repairs and maintenance of many essential activities in a defense period all require 100 per cent allocations.

Furthermore, the uneven spread of defense contracts among firms may call for some unevenness in the curtailments of civilian use of materials, in order to preserve the civilian economy as well as possible. For example, in the case of a material with a very large defense take, spreading cutbacks on civilian use equally might produce such a low rate of operation as to require numerous shutdowns where satisfactory substitute materials were not available. Here, it would be better for the long-run vigor of the civilian economy, including the prevention of unemployment or unneces-

---

skills in very short supply. But in such a case it would seem more appropriate to prohibit or limit the use in specified civilian work of the type of skilled worker that must be transferred to military production.

sary migration of labor, to give more of the material to firms that could do little defense business, in order to keep them in civilian production. Defense contracts should be spread as broadly as possible but there will probably be need for special provisions for small businesses and for industries and districts not well equipped to handle much defense work.[15]

To protect small business, which is usually at a disadvantage in obtaining materials in short supply, controls must be tight enough so that permitted claims or demands for a material do not exceed the amount available—in other words, so that all can find suppliers to sell them the amounts to which they are entitled. The control agency also can reserve a "kitty" from which to dole out supplies in cases of special need. The very small users can be exempted from controls without endangering the program.

With these qualifications, the principle of equality of treatment in restricting civilian use of scarce materials seems desirable in the defense period. This principle also will tend to keep in production a wide range of civilian goods, although the various items may not be available in exactly the relative volume desired by consumers.

But in the case of durable goods, where cutbacks chiefly apply, consumer stocks of relatively new articles have been high. In such a situation the pattern of cutbacks would not, within broad limits, greatly impair consumer satisfaction—

15. The armed services have been holding prime contractor-subcontractor clinics all over the country to bring together large contractors and small plant operators. The Small Defense Plants Administration was organized to give special attention to increasing the contribution of small business to the defense effort. The Departments of Defense and Commerce have held "on the spot" industry-assistance programs in seriously affected industrial areas to give firms affected by cutbacks information on possibilities for prime or subcontracts in defense work. *Fourth Quarterly Report of the Director of Defense Mobilization*, January 1, 1952, p. 25.

unless government allocation should last more than a few years. For the health and vigor of our economy, it is more important in a short period to see that every established producer has a fair opportunity to continue in business while controls are in effect than to try to meet precisely the patterns of consumer demand. This in fact will serve consumers best over the long term.

Two Contrasting Views

The judgment here expressed differs from two fairly common views. One is that meeting the pattern of consumer demands at all times is the most important end of the economic system. The other view is that there should be a central determination of all degrees of essentiality of products—just as in full war—whenever there are marked shortages of materials in the defense period, and elimination of the less needed products by the controls.

The first view overlooks the injury to enterprise and competition which could be great enough, even in two or three years, to outweigh a considerable degree of temporary divergence of production from the exact proportions that consumers desire. With marked shortages and no government control of the flow of materials there is no assurance that the available materials will be divided among firms on the basis of relative long-run efficiency in meeting consumer demands. Favoritism and immediate financial capacity of buyers to pay high prices, or to buy up large amounts to hoard, are likely to be important factors. Government control can try to assure all existing users of materials a chance to stay in business until materials are again fairly plentiful and the relative fortunes of firms can be decided in free markets operating under more normal conditions.

What Is Essential?

The second view overlooks the fact that decisions on what is "more" and "less" essential have to be fairly arbitrary until civilian consumption is down at least within speaking distance of wartime minimums—something that is not necessary in a limited defense program. It is hard enough in wartime for high-minded, responsible men to draw lines between degrees of essentiality. In a limited defense program the problem is infinitely more difficult.

In wartime, we cannot afford the luxury of new producers unless they can make munitions or other required items better or more cheaply than can established enterprises. In a long defense period, on the other hand, the normal opportunity to organize new enterprises should be kept open just as far as possible. Not only is the opportunity to start a business an important part of our democratic ideal; new businesses also help keep competition vigorous so that consumers are continuously better served. True, if the shortage of a material is extreme, spreading the very limited supply more thinly to give some to new firms might make it hard for existing producers to keep going. But wherever the take for defense production and defense-supporting activities leaves a fairly large proportion available for ordinary civilian use—say three fifths or more of normal—new firms should be given access to the supply. This might require the control agency to keep a kitty to help new firms if in spite of financial reliability they should have trouble getting on the books of a supplier.

The same is true of new civilian products and new styles or models of existing articles. In full war these are "out." In a long defense period they should be permitted except, again, in cases of extreme shortage.

Of course, some new firms will turn out to be inefficient and some new products no good. Can we afford these wastes so long as there are shortages of materials and manpower? The wise answer seems to be that unless we do, democratic freedoms will suffer and there will be a tendency toward less vigorous competition and less development of new products that better satisfy consumer desires. Shortages and controls should not be permitted to weaken competition or slow up the development of new products. If any limitations on new styles or models are necessary, they should be confined to things like "trim" and "gadgetry," except, of course, where shortages are acute.

No Substitute for Administrative Discretion

An agency that administers channeling controls on mate rials must have broad discretion. As with other controls to deal with complex problems, Congress can only lay down general standards. The possibility of arbitrary action, favoritism and corruption is inherent in the situation. Political safeguards against these are limited. Perhaps better formulas for equitable channeling can be evolved. But we must recognize that mechanical formulas can be just as arbitrary as discretionary decisions—or even more so. In the administration of materials controls, as in other important government activities, there is no substitute for good administrators —able men of scrupulous honesty who understand the problems and have a high sense of public responsibility.

Advisory industry and labor committees and hearings before appeals boards are devices useful in minimizing inequities, favoritism and arbitrary action. The fact that advisory committees and agency officials rarely agree (on the record, at least) should not be taken to mean that such consultation produces no benefits. Experience indicates that with this consultation the regulations are more realistic and equitable and there is better understanding between the agencies and the affected groups.

Similarly, experience with appeals boards in the War Production Board and the Rationing Department of the Office of Price Administration in World War II seems to indicate that this device can help avoid unnecessary inequities and at the same time show businessmen and others that it never is possible to do the job without some inequities.

7. Manpower Control

COMPULSORY ALLOCATION OF MATERIALS is indispensable to a full war production program and, as we have just seen, with less coverage, to a rapid defense build-up. The manpower parallel would be compulsory assignment of civilians to jobs—as is done with military personnel—under a law making all adults (able to work) subject to national service.

Must Civilians Be Assigned to Jobs?

All-out atomic war might require direct assignment of persons to specific jobs (including freezing essential workers in their jobs) on a vast scale, especially if there were extensive destruction of facilities and heavy casualties in major production centers. Even without such damage to production centers, the outbreak of full war would necessitate a quick shift of hosts of workers. The armed services would call up millions of young men and reservists, many from key industrial jobs because modern warfare requires a large number of technicians in the military forces. In essential industries these men would have to be replaced. Defense plants already in operation would jump to two or three shifts. There would be large cutbacks in the output of civilian goods to release facilities, materials and workers for war production. Many workers would have to move to other jobs in other communities. On the other hand, many workers already in essential employment would have to be "frozen" in their jobs.

To get the right workers into the right jobs rapidly (and to keep them there) would be an enormous problem even without heavy bomb damage and loss of life in production centers. Hence, direct assignment under national service might be necessary; with numerous disasters it is almost sure to be. Passage of a national service law to go into effect on declaration of an emergency by Congress or the President is an indispensable part of a readiness defense program.

Do we need compulsory assignment of civilians to jobs in the defense period? The answer is "No," if we make sufficient use of other measures to keep unemployment low, to increase the labor force, to raise labor output, and to induce workers to move voluntarily to jobs where they are most needed. Under each of these headings there are many measures that can help forestall or overcome manpower shortages. These can be carried out largely through incentives, through such normal government activities as aid to housing, through persuasion by area labor-management committees or area interagency government committees, or through controls on production or materials. These measures, which will be outlined in this chapter, would also be of great service in supplementing mandatory manpower allocation in war.

Unlike compulsory assignment to jobs, the measures treated in this chapter are not incompatible with our basic values and institutions. Hence it would be wise to make the largest possible use of them, even in full war, in order to keep the extent of mandatory assignments to the minimum.

The administration of job assignments would raise extremely difficult problems. Unless workers and jobs were well matched, many persons would feel that the manpower policy was limiting their usefulness instead of employing their full capacities. Everyone knows of cases where the armed forces have assigned men with special skills to unskilled jobs and vice versa. A few such cases may help many others who do not like their job assignments to think that their true abilities are not being used. This would weaken compliance with assignment orders, and tend to lower efficiency. At best, efficiency of workers assigned to jobs may be less than at jobs of their own choosing.

Even with highly effective matching of workers and jobs, mandatory job assignment would produce thorny questions. For example, would workers shifted to jobs in a plant with a lower wage scale be forced to take a pay cut? Could workers ordered to move take along or otherwise retain their pension status and seniority rights? Could exemptions be made in cases of acute hardship without impairing willing compliance by the great majority?

Administration of national service in itself would be costly in manpower—and cumbersome.

For a variety of reasons, it is obviously important to use to the full other means of dealing with manpower shortages, especially in the defense period.

Why We Have Manpower Shortages

A defense program creates occupational shortages in particular skills and professions and geographical shortages where defense work is concentrated. At a peak of defense activity there may be a fairly general manpower shortage, although not as severe as in all-out war.

If we had reliable five-to-ten-year estimates of supplies and requirements of the various kinds of manpower needed, most shortages probably could be anticipated and prevented (except, of course, in the first few years of a defense program). Given enough time the manpower supply can be geared to almost any pattern of needs—by abnormal expansion of the labor force, by retraining of workers and redirection of youth training, and by inducements to workers to move to other jobs. It is training that takes time. Many unskilled jobs can be learned in a matter of hours or weeks. But training for skilled jobs often requires two years or more under present apprenticeship practices; and professional training of scientists, engineers and doctors takes much longer.

As explained in Chapter 5, we do not yet have good estimates of defense requirements for the various types of manpower, even for a year or two ahead. Estimates for a longer period would always be subject to change because of the development of new weapons, changes in strategy or in the underlying international situation. But estimates of minimum "regular" defense requirements could provide guide lines for training larger numbers of the professional and skilled workers most likely to be needed.

Advance preparation of supervisors and trainers would reduce the duration of shortages. And the demand for certain trained personnel—for example, doctors, tool and die makers, electronics and chemical engineers—would probably not be much affected even by substantial changes in strategy or weapons. Here estimates of requirements for several years ahead could be very useful. Even in the absence of precise estimates, however, it is evident that during the defense period more individuals should be trained in skills useful both to defense and to civilian activities.

There is a general manpower shortage only when demand for all kinds of manpower exceeds the available supply, that is, when there is general inflationary pressure throughout the economy. In this situation, most firms will want more workers at current wages than they can get—and more materials, too. General inflationary pressure usually reflects large government deficits, or easy bank credit, or both. A large government deficit is probably inevitable in full war. Some deficit may be unavoidable at the peak of a defense hump. But for most of the defense period it should be possible to prevent the general inflationary pressure that arises from a government deficit, and to make credit control so stringent that bank credit does not stimulate general inflationary demand.

Expansion of the labor force and the resulting increase in output in themselves will not counter general inflationary pressure and excess demand for labor. The incomes earned by added workers swell total spending power.[1] In the last analysis, a general manpower shortage can be prevented or eliminated only by fiscal and monetary controls—taxes high enough and government spending low enough, taken together with current saving by businesses and individuals and strong credit controls, to relieve general inflationary pressure.[2]

This does not, of course, diminish the importance of a larger-than-normal increase in the labor force in the defense period. Such an increase will help deal with particular occupational and geographical manpower shortages. Furthermore, the greater the increase in the labor force, the larger can be the quantity and variety of civilian consumption, the volume of nondefense business investment, including development of new products, and the normal activities of the state, local, and federal governments, including new or improved highways, education and social services.

1. A detailed discussion of this point is given by Albert G. Hart in *Defense without Inflation,* pp. 60-62.

2. With the outbreak of full war it would be desirable to have some general inflationary pressure to induce rapid expansion of the labor force. The same might be true in a sudden emergency in the defense period, if a very large and swift expansion of the labor force was imperative. But most of the time during the defense period we can probably meet our manpower needs without general inflationary pressure.

TABLE 7

ESTIMATES OF LABOR FORCE, EMPLOYMENT AND
UNEMPLOYMENT, FOURTH QUARTER 1950
(ACTUAL), AND FOURTH QUARTERS
1951 AND 1952 (PROJECTED)

(*In Millions*)

Group	Fourth Quarter of:		
	1950	*1951*	*1952*
Total labor force	65.2	67.5	68.4
Unemployed	2.1	1.5	1.5
Employed (including armed forces)	63.1	66.0	66.9
Defense	4.8	9.7	12.0
Armed forces	1.9[a]	3.5	3.5
Civilians	2.9[b]	6.2	8.5
Nondefense	58.3	56.3	54.9

Source: Bureau of Labor Statistics, "Projected Manpower Requirements and
Supply for the Defense Program, 1951-52," Manpower Report No. 7, June
1951, p. 2 (mimeographed).

a. From Council of Economic Advisers, *Annual Economic Review,* January
1952, p. 177.

b. Computed from the figures above.

Defense Manpower Needs and Ways to Meet Them

A large increase in defense requirements will obviously
mean an increase in defense manpower needs. Let us look at
some illustrative figures. In June 1951 the Bureau of Labor
Statistics presented estimates of the increase in defense
manpower needs and in the labor force—persons 14 years
old or over working or seeking work—between the fourth
quarter of 1950 and the fourth quarter of 1952. (See Table
7.) The estimates were based on the production goals outlined in the *First Quarterly Report of the Director of Defense Mobilization* (April 1, 1951) and on the military
manpower goal of 3.5 million scheduled by the Department
of Defense. (The manpower goal for the armed forces is
given as 3.7 million by June 30, 1953 in the *Fifth Quarterly*

Report of the Director of Defense Mobilization, April 1, 1952, p. 2.)

The total increase in manpower needed for defense in the two-year period was estimated as 7.2 million persons, including the build-up of military personnel and the rise in requirements for defense production and transportation, mining and other defense-supporting activities.

The Bureau of Labor Statistics suggested that the additional 7.2 million persons for defense could be supplied in three ways:

(1) Reduction of unemployment to 1.5 million would put 600,000 more men and women to work.

(2) The labor force could be increased by 3.2 million workers. The normal increase, reflecting population growth, return of veterans into the labor market, rising employment of women and other factors, was estimated to be 1.8 million, or 900,000 a year. The Bureau of Labor Statistics held that greater use of women, youth and older workers and better use of the handicapped could provide *in toto* the equivalent of 1.4 million additional workers.[3]

(3) Transfer to defense production from civilian output could supply 3.4 million workers. A large proportion of these

3. Bureau of Labor Statistics, "Projected Manpower Requirements and Supply for the Defense Program, 1951-52," Manpower Report No. 7, June 1951, p. 3 (mimeographed). It is estimated that our labor force will grow by an annual average of 1 million (or a little more or a little less) in the twenty-five years between 1950 and 1975, if the trend of the past three decades continues and work patterns of the population are not radically altered by a major war or other disaster. See Harold Wool, "Long-Term Projections of the Labor Force," a paper presented before the Conference on Income and Wealth of the National Bureau of Economic Research, May 25, 1951, p. 23a (mimeographed). Wool estimates the twenty-five-year growth as somewhere between 22 and 28 million, depending on different assumptions with respect to fertility rates. The normal increase in the labor force will probably be below average in the first half of the 1950s because of the low birth rate in the 1930s. A sharp rise is due in the late 1950s and early 1960s, reflecting the war and postwar baby booms.

would become available automatically as auto producers and others undertook defense work and reduced civilian output.

Actually the total labor force seems to have grown by about 1.8 million, or the estimated normal increase, between December 1950 and December 1952, instead of the 3.2 million suggested by the Bureau of Labor Statistics. In 1951 and 1952 about 1.4 million persons went into the armed forces, so the civilian labor force increased by only about 0.4 million. (See Table 8.) Employment in defense work rose from about 2 million at the time of the Korean outbreak to 5.5 million at the end of 1951 and about 6 million by April 1952.[4]

TABLE 8

DISTRIBUTION OF THE LABOR FORCE,[a]
DECEMBER 1950, 1951 AND 1952
(*In Millions*)

Group	December 1950	December 1951	December 1952
Total labor force	64.7	66.0	66.5
Civilian labor force	62.5	62.7	62.9
Unemployed	2.2	1.7	1.4
Armed forces	2.2	3.3	3.6

Source: Council of Economic Advisers, *Annual Economic Review,* January 1952, p. 177, and January 1953, pp. 83 and 177.
a. Persons aged 14 years and over.

Although the Bureau of Labor Statistics figures overestimated employment in defense work (probably reflecting production goals higher than actual output), they point to three of the principal means of meeting increased demand for defense workers—reduction of unemployment, expansion of the labor force, and shifts from nondefense work to defense

4. *Fifth Quarterly Report of the Director of Defense Mobilization,* April 1, 1952, p. 32.

employment. Another principal means is more effective use of labor.

Reducing Unemployment

In 1944, unemployment fell to about two thirds of a million, or 1.2 per cent of the civilian labor force. This was the result of the extraordinary pressures of a great war effort. Probably this cannot be duplicated in a long defense period, but unemployment can be kept low most of the time.

At the time of the Korean outbreak, unemployment stood at 3.4 million or about 5 per cent of the civilian labor force. It quickly fell below 2.5 million and since March 1951 it has been between 1.6 and 1.9 million most of the time, equivalent to 2.5 to 3 per cent of the civilian labor force.

In the kind of defense period treated in this book, it seems unlikely that unemployment will often go above 5 per cent or below 2 per cent. It may vary between 2.5 and 4 per cent most of the time. With a civilian labor force of 61 million—about the average for 1952—this range would be 1.5-2.4 million persons.

Simply to offer defense jobs takes a good many off the list of the unemployed. But more can be done by making sure that it is known widely what jobs are open, where to apply for them and how to get any necessary training or retraining. It also helps to locate new plants and to place defense contracts in areas that usually have a labor surplus. Unemployment can be cut most easily when workers do not have to move and the problems of additional housing and community services do not arise.

If the unemployed must go to another locality for a job there may be a problem of inadequate housing or community services. For example, in the present defense build-up a considerable slice of the aircraft program was assigned to Wichita, Kansas, in the belief that manpower was available from the surrounding area. It was—but many who came in and started work soon left because of poor housing. In San Diego, California, the basic community facilities, such as water supply, fell short of the needs of the enlarged population called for by expansion of the aircraft industry and activities at military installations.[5]

Increasing the Labor Force

Adding More Women

In World War II about 8 million persons took jobs who would not normally have been in the labor force.[6] About half of these were women. Two million were teen-age boys who went into the armed forces or into productive work. The rest, about 1.8 million, were men who would normally have been considered too old or otherwise unfit to work.

In a defense period we do not want increased use of young people except in military training, or in part-time work that will not interfere with their normal education and training. In the urgency of total war, education often has to be sacrificed. But maintenance of normal education is a pillar of strength in a defense effort. Indeed, the growing need for doctors, scientists, engineers, and some types of skilled workers calls for more training for more young people even though that will delay their entry into the labor force. Hence, if extra workers are needed, we should look to other sources.

We do not want to lower the birth rate or lessen child care and household operation during the defense period, if

5. These two illustrations are given in the *Fourth Quarterly Report of the Director of Defense Mobilization*, January 1, 1952, p. 33.

6. Bureau of Labor Statistics, *Fact Book on Manpower*, January 31, 1951, p. B-1.

only because these would reduce our defense potential as time went on. It would be a mistake to have more than the usual proportion of women between 20 and 35 at work outside their homes. But millions of women beyond this age group not in the labor force could take jobs. At the end of 1950, there were 12 million women between 35 and 55 not in the labor force.[7] Girls between 14 and 20 not attending school made up another million. Many of these women may not want to go to work and many others may be willing to work only part time. Even so, the equivalent of a few million full-time workers could come from this source without limiting child care or homemaking and without reducing substantially the very valuable unpaid civic, charitable and religious activities to which many women devote much time.

In contrast, there were fewer than 10 million males aged 14 and over who were not already in the labor force at the end of 1950; about 4 million of these were in school and 3 million were 65 or over. However, these figures indicate appreciable potential additions to the labor force from this source.

Use of More Older People

Older people who will stay at work a few years longer than they intended can also enlarge the labor force. To those who would not know what to do with themselves after retirement, continued work and responsibility may be a blessing, safeguarding both their happiness and their health.[8]

---

7. *Ibid.*, p. B-4. These figures exclude the small numbers in institutions, disabled or retired. Of the total number of females 14 years of age and over, 19 million were in the labor force and 38 million outside. The number of women 14 and over in the labor force grew between 1940 and 1949 from 13.8 to 17.2 million, an increase from 27.4 to 30.7 per cent. (*Ibid.*, p. C-2.)

8. This seems to be the opinion of many sociologists.

More Use of Handicapped Persons

There probably are at least 2 million handicapped persons who might be retrained to join the labor force or for more productive work.[9] More use of the handicapped is to their own good and to that of the nation.

Better information about job openings and more attention by business and government to working conditions and training or retraining will expand the labor force. If the worker and his family have to move to take a new job, they will be influenced by the housing situation and the quality and quantity of community services—schooling, medical care and recreational facilities as well as the usual public utilities.

Expansion of the labor force through increased use of women, older workers and the handicapped need bring no undesirable results when it comes from voluntary decisions of individuals in response to normal inducements, better information about jobs, provision of good working conditions, training or retraining, and adequate housing and community services. Indeed the result may be to raise levels of well-being for some above those of ordinary peacetime.

More Use of Foreign Labor

The labor force could also be increased by immigration. Larger quotas would bring in more workers, including displaced persons. Our immigration policy sometimes may need to take defense requirements into account, especially the shortage of special skills.

Another way to utilize foreign manpower is to shift some munitions production abroad to areas with ample labor sup-

9. Estimate by the Task Force on Mobilization of the Handicapped, established by the Director of Defense Mobilization. See *Fourth Quarterly Report of the Director of Defense Mobilization*, January 1, 1952, p. 30.

plies. For example, some tanks might be made in Milan, Italy, instead of Detroit. Such a spread of arms production would encourage responsibility for defense in other lands and a sense of teamwork among the free nations. Also, it might replace economic aid that would otherwise be necessary to maintain the economic strength of other countries. However, to place critical munitions production in vulnerable locations involves questions of military security which often outweigh political and economic policy.

Raising Labor Output

We can raise the output of a given labor force by: (1) reducing "underemployment" of minority groups and rural workers; (2) improving technology, organization and administration; (3) training workers for more productive jobs and redesigning jobs; (4) lessening labor hoarding; (5) lowering absenteeism and turnover; (6) lengthening the work week.

Use of "Underemployed" Workers

Some members of minority groups (racial, religious or national) are not working at jobs that use their full capacities, because of discrimination in hiring, lack of opportunity for training, or other barriers. Better use of these "underemployed" workers would obviously increase the output of the labor force. In some instances, more efficient use of these individuals is more difficult to achieve than more general use of women, older people and the handicapped, owing to the prejudices of fellow workers, of management, or both. Much can be accomplished, however, by statesmanlike unions and managements, with or without local labor-management committees, by civic leaders, and by sound administration of state and municipal measures against discrimination.[10]

"Underemployment" also seems to be substantial in many rural areas in various parts of the country.[11] A number of farmers and farm laborers are operating below efficient standards because the farms are too small, the land too poor, or their methods backward. Many of these could leave agriculture without materially affecting total farm production. Their use in industry, or in more effective farm operation, would raise national production.

In World War II, these areas were a rich source of labor for defense plants. For example, workers from rural areas in

10. The figures below suggest the order in which a number of business companies rate the sources of additional workers. The proportion of companies intending to hire larger numbers of Negroes is substantial although lower than the proportion intending to hire more women, older persons and handicapped workers.

Source of Manpower for Present Emergency

	Smaller Companies	Larger Companies
Will hire increased numbers of women........	67 per cent	81 per cent
Will hire increased numbers of older workers (over 50)	57	68
Will hire increased numbers of handicapped workers	48	54
Will hire increased numbers of Negroes.......	28	46
Other	20	22

The figures are a tabulation of replies to the question: "In securing new workers for the present emergency, will you rely on increased hiring of (a) women (b) persons over 50 years old (c) Negroes (d) handicapped workers (e) others?" The questionnaire was sent at the end of January 1951, by the Bureau of National Affairs of Washington, D.C., to each of 160 personnel and industrial relations officials who were members of the 1951 panel of BNA, Personnel Policies Forum. The question seems to overlook the use of older people through keeping them after normal retirement age.

11. *Underemployment of Rural Families; Materials Prepared for the Joint Committee on the Economic Report by the Committee Staff,* Joint Committee Print, 82d Cong., 1st sess., 1951.

Tennessee and Kentucky helped man bag-loading plants in Virginia and Indiana and war plants in Ohio and Michigan. In this defense period more effective use of "underemployed" rural manpower could step up national output.

Improving Technology, Organization and Administration

In normal times, output per man-hour has increased in the United States at an average rate of about 2½ per cent a year for the economy as a whole. This has been the result of continuous technological progress in industry and agriculture and of better organization and administration of production and marketing and services.

In the defense period, we should be able to raise the rate of increase in man-hour productivity if we redouble our efforts. Wherever new plants are needed for defense or defense-supporting activities, the most modern and efficient equipment can be installed.[12] Expansion of capacity for defense production—materials, intermediate products and end items—offers an opportunity for continuous advance in average productivity of the whole economy at a rate above that of normal peacetime. Metals, chemicals, machine tools, petroleum, power, transportation and the like, which are included in defense and defense-supporting production, make up a very substantial part of the whole economy.

Improvements in technology, organization and administration are particularly the job of management with aid from labor. In the case of small business and farming, however, advice and guidance from government, along with financial aid where it is needed, can help promote the maximum advance.

12. Although regular business investment for nondefense purposes may have to be curtailed somewhat in hump periods, most of this cut can probably be made up in nonhump periods, and perhaps all of it.

Improving Skills and Redesigning Jobs

Man-hour productivity can be raised in many cases by better training of workers. Many members of the labor force are being used on jobs below their capacity. They lack the necessary training because of inertia, meager opportunity, limited means or some other cause.

Training handicapped persons to increase their productivity was treated above as a special case (under the heading of increasing the labor force) since many of them are not employable without training.

Both management and labor can help improve in-plant training to make better use of the labor already employed. Government—local, state and federal—can aid schools and vocational institutes in improving and broadening training programs.

Where a shortage of skilled labor cannot be met by training additional skilled workers, the job can sometimes be redesigned and broken down into operations that semiskilled or unskilled labor can handle.

Lessening the Hoarding of Labor

Manpower shortages breed a natural inclination in plant managers to hoard labor—that is, to hire more men than are actually needed at the moment in anticipation of additional orders or rising labor turnover. The result is idle labor, at least part of the time. To the extent that this practice is prevented or lessened, total output obviously will be larger.

Good results can often be obtained by voluntary agreement to respect the requests or guiding rules of local labor-management committees or government agencies. However, if manpower shortages threaten serious harm to defense production, the federal government should have the power to impose "inventory control" over manpower as well as materials and parts. This control would take the form of setting a ceiling on the amount of manpower a plant could hire. Manpower ceilings would not curb to any serious degree the freedom of choice of individuals or managements. Any firm that wanted to help get maximum production by refraining from labor hoarding would benefit from government control forcing others to do likewise.

Lowering Absenteeism and Turnover

Some supposedly full-time workers "play hooky" a few days each month. This is called absenteeism. Output can be raised by diminishing this, especially where absenteeism creates bottlenecks in particular materials or parts.

Often the best way to lower absenteeism is to improve working conditions in the plant, including recreational facilities. Sometimes, however, it reflects community conditions—inadequate housing, poor transportation, lack of nearby medical facilities, recreational opportunities or shops. Management, labor and government all can help improve such conditions.

Labor turnover means the rate at which employees quit and new ones are hired. It takes a little time for new workers to attain efficiency; hence a cut in labor turnover increases output. The causes of high labor turnover seem to parallel those leading to high absenteeism.

Lengthening the Work Week

In full war there must be an increase in the length of the work week everywhere to the point where it fails to add to output, because of reduced efficiency, increased absenteeism, high turnover or the like. Lengthening the work week may also be necessary in the case of shortages of critical items in the defense period, especially during production humps.

Wherever defense needs can be met by expansion of plant capacity, increase in the labor force, or raising man-hour output, instead of lengthening the work week, this will increase the potential expansion of output in the event of full war. The case is similar to that of expanding capacity to meet defense demand without the use of double or triple shifts, although quantitatively it is less important.

To avoid lengthening the work week, except where shortages demand it, is also in line with the aim of keeping the civilian economy as healthy as possible. In a long defense period, it is undesirable to curtail substantially the time men and women normally give to homemaking, recreation, participation in community affairs, adult education, and other activities that contribute both to personal and public well-being in a democracy.

In general, the length of the work week can be left to labor and management with some guidance from defense agencies. However, if adequate production of items of critical importance for defense is found to be impaired by failure to stretch the work week, the government should be given legal authority to require a reasonable lengthening on a finding of a specific emergency which otherwise could not be resolved.

Influencing the Allocation of Labor

A limited defense program, like full mobilization, requires both geographical movement of some labor and change in the proportions of different types of labor or skills. There often are strong deterrents to geographical shifts—inadequate housing, schooling or other community services, loss of seniority rights or of special retirement benefits. Hence it is desirable to "take the work to the workers" wherever that can be done.

A defense program calls for large numbers of skilled metal, electronics and chemical workers, tool and die makers, scientists, engineers and many other kinds of skilled craftsmen and technicians. These are needed both to meet current demands for defense production and to ensure readiness for full mobilization. Until much larger numbers can be trained, the persons who already have these skills must be reallocated to some extent.

Taking the Work to the Workers

In the latter part of World War II, local manpower shortages developed in a number of labor markets. Study of the situation showed that these shortages reflected in part the practice of procurement authorities in placing contracts largely with particular companies or in particular localities having a good record on specific types of work. With many companies in the same area counting on the same supplies of labor, power, housing and so on, shortages quickly developed. In spite of efforts to move labor into these areas, the shortages continued, even though many areas had some surplus manpower or underemployment. From this experience we learned the importance of placing contracts in areas with labor surplus, including underemployed labor.

An initial defense build-up calls for expansion of capacity for defense production and defense-supporting activities, and later humps may do the same. The new plants should be located in areas that have relatively greater supplies of the needed kinds of labor and that would be among the less tight areas in full mobilization; or in areas where the needed labor supplies can be obtained by retraining workers in less essential civilian industries or from underemployed manpower there or in nearby rural areas. In general, this means keeping new plants out of large, thriving centers of industry and population.

Needless to say, temporary unemployment of labor fitted for defense work, such as existed in Detroit in late 1951 and early 1952, would not indicate that an area would be among the less tight in full mobilization.

To take new plants to the workers obviously requires knowledge of where there are unemployed or underemployed persons to man them. This information has to be given to procurement officers and to the companies that are going to build the plants. The policy's success also requires guiding rules for procurement officers, and for the officials allocating materials for new plants and handling accelerated amortization and government loans and loan guarantees.

Some defense contracts may be placed with companies which will use part of their existing facilities and labor force on defense work. Automobile companies and producers of other consumer durable goods have trained metal workers, electrical workers and others with skills needed in munitions production. This way of taking the work to the workers lessens intercompany shifts and reduces problems of seniority, pensions and other benefits.

Taking the work to the workers does not altogether avoid increased needs for housing, schools and other community services. But since many workers can continue to live in the same homes and use the same schools, transportation and other services these problems are lessened as compared with bringing in throngs of new workers to man new plants. Also, it may be easier to persuade workers to commute or move into a nearby center than to induce them to pull up roots and go to a strange and faraway city.

Increasing Supplies of Particular Skills

It is a truism to say that the cure for acute shortage is to increase supply. In the case of manpower, this means training larger numbers in the skills needed in defense production. Many unskilled and semiskilled workers can learn new defense jobs quickly and easily. Training of skilled workers takes more time and requires expansion of in-plant training programs and vocational training in educational institutions. The cooperation of management and labor can help enlarge the number of trainees and shorten the time of training.

More scientists and engineers are needed not only for the military part of our defense program but also for foreign aid programs.[13] World War II demonstrated the military advantage of rapid developments in science and engineering and their application to weapons, not only in the most dramatic instance—the atomic bomb—but in countless other cases. To assure the success of our foreign aid and development programs we shall have to provide at first many persons with scientific and engineering skills. Persons equipped to design educational and training programs for underdeveloped countries also will be indispensable. In international relations we need more men and women trained in the social sciences and in public affairs. Furthermore, rapid increases in productivity in industry and agriculture at home—advances that can provide both more guns and more butter—

13. See Robert L. Clark, Director, Manpower Office, National Security Resources Board, lecture at Indiana University, April 11, 1951, pp. 6 ff. (mimeographed). Several of the following points in the text were made by Mr. Clark in this lecture.

depend heavily on a growing supply of trained manpower in physical science, engineering and administration.

Skilled and professional workers ordinarily get higher-paid and more interesting jobs. Hence it should not be difficult to induce larger numbers of qualified persons to undertake such training, given available programs and financial assistance to those who need it. However, many universities seem to lack adequate facilities and staffs for enlarged graduate training in medicine, in natural and social sciences, and in engineering. And some very promising young men and women are unable to obtain graduate training because they cannot afford it out of their own means and there are not enough fellowships to go around. To expand graduate training programs will probably require additional state or federal funds, or both.

Freeing Labor from Nonessential Activities

In full war, only the most essential activities can be permitted. In the defense period we want as many civilian goods and services as are consistent with the needed defense program. Hence, in this period there should be few, if any, orders restricting the uses of manpower. However, there may be instances, especially in hump periods, where such orders are unavoidable.

Labor can be freed from nonessential activities for defense work by two kinds of order. One is the production limitation order, described in the preceding chapter, which prohibits or limits output of a product and thus frees facilities and materials, as well as labor.

In full war such orders are necessary wherever it is important to convert plants and their manpower complements to war production. In a defense program, a few of these orders may be needed in an initial rapid build-up or a similar build-up later. But their extensive or continued use in a defense period would be inconsistent with the aim of maintaining balanced production of the things consumers want and freedom to businessmen to turn out whatever they think their markets demand.

When the need is to free a portion of certain kinds of labor for defense uses, this can be accomplished by a conservation order prohibiting specified, nonessential uses of such labor, or restricting the numbers employed in each of these uses to a stated percentage of those so employed in a base period. This would be the counterpart of the materials conservation orders described in Chapter 6. Such an order would save from shutdown the firms that could redesign jobs to use less skilled labor, and hence save their other workers from being thrown out of a job.

It would leave to the individual workers released for transfer a substantial range of free choice of occupation, even though they were guided by referral and labor priorities to the jobs where they were most needed.[14] However, even such conservation orders should be used only if there is no other way to induce enough workers to shift to defense production.

Inducing Workers to Change Jobs

Even after the best that can be done in taking the work to the workers and training larger numbers for particular needs, some geographical and intercompany movement of labor will be required. In the case of acute shortages orders

---

14. Cf. Clark, *op. cit.*, p. 12. Moreover, orders limiting output of specified products rather than certain uses of manpower may not release much skilled labor because employers are often willing to incur expense to retain their skilled force for permitted civilian work or anticipated defense work. *Ibid.*, p. 10.

restricting the use of the scarce manpower, just discussed, may have to be used to facilitate shifts.

The principal measures to induce shifts of manpower geographically or company-wise or both are evident on examination of the chief deterrent factors: lack of information on defense job opportunities and working conditions in other areas and on housing, transportation and community services there; ownership of a home; doubt whether housing in defense job areas will be as satisfactory; uncertainty as to transportation and other important community services—health and medical care, schools and recreation facilities; loss or fear of loss of seniority rights, retirement benefits, or other advantages under present labor contracts; expense of moving; fear of inferior working conditions or reduction in wages. Some of these, such as loss of seniority and pension benefits, often accompany a job change from one company to another in the same area.

If these deterrents can be overcome many workers will move to defense jobs in other areas, without compulsory assignment. Here the government must take principal responsibility, for only government can assemble full information on employment needs (job opportunities), and only government can do the things necessary to bring about quick expansion of housing and community services. Such expansion often requires effective cooperation of federal, state and local governments.

Preservation of seniority, retirement and other benefits in existing status or labor contracts may require legislation, if it is to be made general for all workers who transfer to defense work in other companies. As a general rule, business does not recompense workers for moving expenses, but government can.

Removing Further Deterrents to Job Shifts

Managements of plants in need of more workers for defense jobs can maintain high standards in working conditions—a most important measure.

Wage rates on defense jobs should be equivalent to the higher rates for the same or similar work on other jobs in the same section.[15] Managements and unions can cooperate in establishing such wage rates where they do not exist. In most cases, increases above these levels will not be needed if the other steps already sketched are taken; and they would jeopardize stabilization and also interfere with the desirable reallocation of labor in the section by disrupting existing wage relationships more or less all along the line.

Both management and labor can urge government to do its part of the indispensable "other steps," outlined above. In World War II, many employers did not see the need for these or for stabilization. They assumed that they could get more labor by raising wages and nothing more. This also seemed the natural procedure to many wage earners, union and nonunion. But wage-rate premiums large enough to move workers at an abnormally rapid rate, in the absence of those "other steps," are probably larger than needed to *hold* the additional workers once they are moved. As collective bargaining works, however, these rates seldom would go down. The result would be disruption of wage relationships in the area and inflationary increases all along the line

15. The term "section" here means a fairly large region within which many workers can be induced to move around. Examples are New England, the Pacific Northwest, and the section that includes the cities of New York, Trenton, Philadelphia, Wilmington and Baltimore with adjoining communities and areas. A section of the country will usually include several of the 174 major labor market "areas" (many of which are individual cities) for which the U.S. Department of Labor reports current labor shortages or surpluses.

to correct the maladjustments and inequities—unless firm wage control prevented the original inflationary wage boosts or the ensuing adjustments. If they will, managements and unions can prevent this confusion in the defense period or in another war.

Resort to Labor Priorities

Where manpower shortages are substantial, labor priorities—that is, ratings of the relative importance of the various critical labor needs—should be established by a federal interagency committee of production and manpower authorities. Labor exchanges (local, state or federal) should then urge all qualified applicants to take the jobs with the higher priorities. In the defense period, state employment exchanges may be able to cope well enough with area shortages. In full war they would probably have to be absorbed into a federal employment service, to assure reallocations of manpower with maximum effectiveness.

If government restrictions on use of scarce kinds of manpower prove necessary, then government should also follow through and make sure, as far as possible, that the released manpower goes where it is most needed.[16] An effective program means the use of one set of labor priorities by all public labor exchanges, energetic efforts by these exchanges to guide manpower into the most critical jobs, and energetic efforts by governments, managements and unions to remove deterrents to the flow of labor to the points where it is most needed.

16. The gold mines were shut down in World War II by government order with the purpose of providing more labor for nonferrous metal mines. Apparently little of this labor went into the nonferrous mines and its distribution among other occupations was not ascertained.

The National Manpower Mobilization Policy of 1951

The President promulgated on January 17, 1951 a National Manpower Mobilization Policy, basic provisions of which were stated as follows:[17]

a. The size of the armed forces will be determined by the President. He will be provided with the Department of Defense requirements to meet strategic plans; with full information on the prospective supplies of manpower, and on the manpower requirements for defense production, agriculture, civil defense, and other essential purposes.

b. The greatest care must be exercised to assure that the supply of persons possessing critical skills will be distributed among military and civilian activities in a manner which will contribute most to the mobilization program. When the total need for workers with critical skills for civilian and military assignments is expected to exceed the supply that can be made available, the requirements for persons with such skills will be reviewed and distribution of the supply will be measured by the relative urgency of the need for critical skills as between the armed forces and the civilian economy.

c. Policies in respect to recruitment of individuals from civilian life and call-up members of the unorganized reserves will have as their objective the use of persons possessing irreplaceable skills where they can make their maximum contribution to the total mobilization program.

d. Policies governing occupational deferment of persons subject to induction under the Selective Service Act, will provide for: (1) the occupational deferment of persons possessing critical skills if they are currently using such skills in essential activities, except to the extent the military services require persons with these skills; (2) deferment of a sufficient number of individuals in educational and training institutions to provide an adequate continuing supply of professional and highly skilled manpower.

e. Recruitment, placement, distribution, training and utilization of the civilian labor force (including government employees) will be

17. U.S. Department of Labor, *National Manpower Mobilization Policy,* pp. 5-10.

based primarily upon voluntary measures for manpower mobilization. This policy will be carried out through such measures as: (1) providing appropriate employment information to guide workers to jobs in which they can make their maximum contribution; (2) developing recruitment and rehabilitation activities needed to expand the labor force; (3) training persons to meet civilian manpower requirements and providing appropriate placement services; (4) providing assistance to employers in promoting maximum utilization of the labor force including women, physically handicapped, older workers, and minority groups; (5) providing adequate housing and community services; and (6) assisting workers to arrange for their transfer to essential jobs in other areas.

f. Government manpower controls will be used when and to the extent needed to assure successful execution of the mobilization program. Such controls will apply to employers, to workers, or to both. They will include (1) restricting indiscriminate labor turnover through control of separations; (2) giving effect to manpower allocations by placing employment ceilings on employers with respect to the total number of workers, the number of men or the number in particular skills; (3) controlling of employer hiring, and (4) enforcing adherence to utilization standards, including full use of women, handicapped workers, and minority groups.

g. All manpower programs will be geared to the needs and problems of specific geographical areas.

h. As mutually desirable to the United States and friendly nations, workers will be brought into the United States for, or their services utilized within the borders of their own country on, work of value to the mobilization program. Full use of domestic manpower resources will be made before bringing in foreign workers.

i. Production will be scheduled, materials allocated, and procurement distributed with careful consideration of available manpower. Whenever feasible from an economic and security standpoint, production facilities, contracts, and significant subcontracts will be located at the sources of labor supply in preference to moving the labor supply.

j. The full understanding and assistance of labor organizations, employer associations, professional societies, civic and community groups, and State and local governments will be sought in carrying out these functions.

k. Each department will, itself, implement the policy and be responsible for its supervision.

The Director of Defense Mobilization issued Defense Manpower Policy statement No. 1, effective August 2, 1951, to carry out paragraph i above. Thereafter, a Department of Defense Directive was issued (October 19, 1951) to instruct procurement officers how to carry out this policy.[18]

These policy statements and directives, which include a number of the points set forth in this chapter, seem to be on the right track. Subsequent Manpower Policy statements dealt with other points, such as more extensive use of older workers, more effective use and more training of scientific and technical personnel, measures to hold skilled workers in agriculture, and placement of procurement contracts in areas with substantial unemployment.

In July 1952, the Director of Defense Mobilization recommended to management (with the cooperation of labor) "a set of employment principles designed to fulfill on a voluntary basis our manpower needs and requirements," developed by the national Labor-Management Manpower Policy Committee, composed of labor and management representatives.[19] These principles called for employing only the minimum number for the job, nondiscriminatory hiring, cooperation with the Federal-State Employment Service to make the fullest use of manpower, pre-employment training facilities and extension of in-plant training, use of local labor to the fullest possible extent, participation with community groups in

18. Department of Defense Directive, Title 250 Supply Management, Number 250.03-10.

19. *Sixth Quarterly Report of the Director of Defense Mobilization,* July 1, 1952, p. 27.

dealing with problems of housing, school and recreational facilities and other community services, reduction of absenteeism and turnover, and cooperation with area labor-management manpower policy committees to work out solutions for area problems.

Draft Deferment and Manpower Shortages

In full war, deferment from military service should depend primarily on occupational status rather than on the number of dependents. It is easier for government to provide supplemental allowances to take care of the children of a racetrack attendant than to provide a replacement for the childless electronics engineer who would be drafted if the other man were deferred on account of dependents. It is high time that we viewed the situation realistically and recognized that in war irreplaceable workers in munitions plants, metal mines, research laboratories and the many other essential war-supporting activities are just as important as personnel of the armed forces—and that dependency status is irrelevant to the maximizing of the war effort.

In a long defense period, the general rule should be that all able-bodied young men should receive substantial military training. This can be so arranged that boys usually are drafted as they leave school or college. Given this general practice, it would seem desirable to have deferment from the draft and from recall of reserves (except in a serious emergency), on grounds of dependents, for men beyond the normal age for initial military training—say over 25. This would discourage as little as possible the rearing of normal families.

In the defense period, draft deferment should be used to help overcome manpower shortages only when production or manpower authorities certify an acute shortage of a specific skill or professional training. When there is an acute shortage of a skill that requires a year or more of training it is unreasonable to take into the armed forces anyone having that skill until the shortage is overcome.[20]

Is it possible to combine universal military service with the training of an adequate number of persons with skills calling for years of training and experience—scientists, engineers, doctors? The answer would seem to be, "Yes, given time and money." One or two years of military service for all young men would obviously set back for one or two years the beginning of advanced training. But after the first group began, the same number could enter such training each year. There seems to be nothing about military training in itself that would lower the number desiring to become scientists, doctors, engineers or the like. More fellowships, or "G.I. benefits," or loans will, of course, be needed, because more students, being older, will be married. This should not be discouraged. There are few better uses of government funds.

Some men may feel that, after taking a year or two out for military training, they cannot afford several years more for full-scale professional training. However, the experience with G.I.'s after World War II strongly suggests that if financial support is adequate the numbers desiring professional training will be large.

On the basis of the foregoing it seems reasonable to conclude that the manpower problems of the defense period can be satisfactorily treated without undesirable institutional change, provided labor, management and government cooperate in the application of a variety of appropriate measures. We should not conclude that this will come about auto-

---

20. This seems to be covered in the *National Manpower Policy* described above. See section d of "Basic Manpower Mobilization Policies."

matically or that it will be easy. Although the needed controls take the form of inducements, guiding rules or goals, or restrictions that leave a considerable area of free choice, they will frequently call for behavior that runs counter to individual habits and preferences.

8. Direct Stabilization Controls Strategy

INFLATION CAN DAMAGE a war production or defense program, no matter how good the production programming and the controls on use of materials, facilities and manpower. These controls can operate successfully only when there is general stability of prices and wages and other income rates.[1] Chronic inflation in a long defense period also could injure basic democratic values and institutions.[2] We have seen that general controls on prices and wage and salary rates are indispensable in full war; and that they will probably be needed at times in a defense period, because fiscal and credit policies cannot cope successfully with large speculative or panic buying, a strong price-wage spiral, or a budget deficit in a brief peak of defense spending. In Chapter 4 we also concluded that general use of these direct controls would probably not be needed at other times—and that they should be promptly removed when the need has passed—provided that we regularly use the right fiscal and credit policies and that business and labor can be relied on to follow noninflationary price and wage policies.

When direct stabilization controls are needed what should they be? Do we have to have the full program of direct wartime controls in the defense period? Or can we get along without some things—such as subsidies and rationing—and with less extensive coverage of price and wage control, less restrictive forms of control, less stringent price and wage standards? Should the extent and tightness of the program be varied from time to time to follow changes in inflationary

1. See p. 70.
2. Chapter 2, *passim.*

168

pressure? How can we hold to a minimum interference with basic free market institutions?

To answer these questions we need to develop a general strategy of direct stabilization controls, which is the job of this chapter, and to give a more detailed examination of price control, rationing and wage control in the following two chapters.

A Full Program of Direct Stabilization Controls

Full war requires a full program of direct stabilization controls. The strongest feasible fiscal measures will still leave a wide inflationary gap between government expenditure and revenue. This probably cannot be closed by government bond sales to the public. Strong direct controls on prices, rents, wages and salaries, and other income rates will be indispensable. The alternative would be galloping inflation, disastrous to the war effort. Materials and labor would be hoarded or otherwise diverted from the war effort. Jumping prices would impair allocation controls and industrial strife would keep output below the maximum. Rapidly rising living costs would weaken the morale of the armed services and of industrial workers.

An upward creep in costs and prices in most industries would be unavoidable in wartime because increases in some prices, rents, or wage and salary rates would be necessary to correct gross inequities, or to facilitate special controls on materials, facilities or manpower designed to obtain increased amounts of essential goods. Furthermore, the substitution of less efficient workers to replace men and women drawn into the armed services often will increase costs, and substitution of higher-cost materials for scarce items will have the same effect.

But the price and wage lines can be held quite closely with an adequate program. This was demonstrated in World War II. Between April 1943, when "hold-the-line" price and wage policies went into effect, and August 1945, when the shooting war ended, wholesale prices increased, on the average, only about 2 per cent, consumer prices about 4 per cent and urban manufacturing wage rates between 10 and 11 per cent.[3] Even adding a few percentage points for factors not fully reckoned in the price indices—disappearance of lower-priced lines or models, quality deterioration and black market prices—it remains true that prices were quite stable in this twenty-nine-month period. Although wage increases in manufacturing were somewhat larger than the price increases, they were relatively small.

This result was achieved by a less than full stabilization program. In another war, inflationary pressure probably would be greater but the stabilization program also could be made stronger.

Must Be Fair to All Major Groups

The fundamental requirement of an effective stabilization program is that it maintain an acceptable balance of interests among the major groups in the country—labor, farmers, business and professional groups—a balance of prices, wages, profits and other incomes. In our kind of society government controls that greatly affect incomes of individuals or groups will work well—even in all-out war—only if the great majority believe the controls are both fair and necessary. There will have to be enforcement on the fringes, but we cannot and do not want to police the public generally.

3. The figures are given by H. M. Douty, "The Development of Wage-Price Policies," Chapter 3 of *Problems and Policies of Dispute Settlement and Wage Stabilization during World War II,* Bulletin No. 1009, Bureau of Labor Statistics, p. 138.

Seven Principal Elements

A full program of direct stabilization controls, such as we need in all-out war or other serious emergency, includes seven major elements:

1. Limitation on the use of price and wage increases as incentives.
2. Reasonable absorption of cost increases.
3. Restrictions on automatic escalation of prices and wages.
4. Differential pricing.
5. Subsidies.
6. Prevention of production shifts from low-price, low-profit items to high-price, high-profit items.
7. Rationing of consumer goods.[4]

1. Use of Price and Wage Increases as Incentives

Extensive use of price and wage increases as incentives to enlarge supplies of essential commodities, to shift workers or to place procurement contracts would keep the price and wage levels in continuous upward movement and heighten inflationary psychology. This would produce the very inflation a stabilization program is supposed to prevent.

To increase supplies of essential commodities, to shift workers and to place procurement contracts, the main reliance must be on direct controls on the use of resources, aided — where necessary — by supplementary payments to cover special costs of diverting materials, facilities or manpower into needed uses, or to cover the extra costs of marginal supplies.

Incentive increases in prices and wage rates should be limited to cases where even the most effective direct controls

---

4. Direct controls on the use of materials, facilities and manpower to prevent all but essential activities will, of course, make illegal large chunks of demand for particular commodities and particular types of labor. Thus they will aid specific price and wage controls (as noted explicitly in discussion of item 6), and could logically be included in the list of direct stabilization controls here.

on use of resources will not work well without them. These cases will occur chiefly in such fields as grains and other farm products where effective controls are especially difficult to work out and administer.

2. *Reasonable Absorption of Cost Increases*

We have noted that in wartime there will be an inevitable upward creep in costs in most industries. Were every cost increase matched by an increase in the ceiling price of the commodity, the price level would be in continuous upward motion. This would be a creeping inflation which would heighten inflationary psychology and threaten a surging price-wage spiral. Administrative authorities probably cannot administer an inflation so as to keep it within tolerable bounds.[5] Hence every industry must be required to absorb cost increases, at least in part, so long as its profits are above a minimum reasonable level. (Standards for reasonable absorption are discussed in the next chapter.)

3. *Restricting Automatic Price and Wage Rises*

In the last few decades automatic adjustments of prices and income rates have become a prominent feature of our economic institutions. Familiar examples are sliding scale adjustments of public utility rates to changes in costs or earnings, parity prices for farm products, and escalator clauses in wage contracts providing for automatic adjustments of wage rates in relation to changes in consumer prices, increases in productivity, or other factors. In many cases business uses cost-plus pricing policies that seem to be more or less automatic.

---

5. If cost increases occurred only for a few commodities it might be sensible to let their prices go up, as in peacetime, to encourage consumers to shift to cheaper things. But with costs increasing nearly everywhere, cost-plus pricing would ensure inflation.

In wartime all such automatic escalators should be suspended "for the duration." As we just saw, cost increases must be absorbed so far as possible. Increases in productivity should go into enlargement of the war effort rather than into wages or profits. Wage increases to match increases in consumer prices should be ruled out, together with increases in farm prices to preserve "parity." True, increases in prices or public utility rates would have to be allowed when cost absorption brought the profits of an industry or utility below a minimum reasonable level. And to maintain a balance of interests among the major groups it might be necessary to permit a partial adjustment of wage rates generally if the cost of living should rise by a substantial amount, say 10 per cent. For the same reason, farm prices might have to be raised somewhat if the average parity ratio fell substantially. But the rule should be no *automatic* adjustments.

4. Differential Pricing

This device means charging different prices for different parts of the supply of a commodity. Peacetime examples are common—the same foods or drugs frequently vary in price in different kinds of retail stores. Manufacturers often charge different prices to different classes of purchaser. When price ceilings are established, existing differential prices will usually be incorporated.

Differential pricing can also be used to hold down the amount of increase permitted in ceiling prices. It would be inflationary to give a price increase across the board on the whole output of oil, or lumber, steel, beef, men's shirts, or Navy uniforms just because producers of 20 or 25 per cent of the supply could not make reasonable returns at established ceiling prices. Furthermore, where expansion of output of a commodity is needed and the cheapest available additional supply will cost too much for profitable production at the regular ceiling price, a higher price for the high-cost part of the supply, but for that alone, is the best policy. Copper, lead, oil, coal and lumber are commodities of which marginal supplies can usually be obtained at higher-than-normal costs.

If differential price increases can be absorbed by processors or at wholesale or retail levels, no increase in price to ultimate consumers (including government) will be necessary. If different prices to buyers of a standard commodity such as copper or steel are not practicable—because they would impair an allocation scheme or for some other reason—government can buy at different prices and resell at a uniform price equal to the average of the purchase price. Where a commodity goes largely into war goods or is very important in living or business costs, there arises the question of replacing differential prices by marginal subsidy payments.

5. Subsidies

In wartime, such commodities as copper and oil are bought largely by the government or go into war goods bought by the government. If the government pays differential prices in the form of direct subsidies to producers of the high-cost marginal supplies of these commodities, meanwhile maintaining the regular ceiling prices on them, there will be a large saving to the government, as compared with across-the-board increases in ceilings that would be passed on to the government. Such payments are not subsidies in the ordinary sense, because they actually save the government money and hold down the public debt.

Government subsidy should also take the place of differential price increases for marginal supplies of important cost-of-living commodities, such as bread, milk, butter and meat, if the increases cannot be absorbed before they reach the consumer. When such subsidy payments permit a tighter rein on wages they save the government money in the end.

Subsidies on important commodities are also justified to cover substantial increases in costs of production, transportation or distribution resulting from war-caused dislocations. Examples in World War II were the war-risk insurance added to ocean shipping costs and the higher cost of rail shipment of oil for domestic use as compared with ocean transport, curtailed by the tanker shortage. Unavoidable war-caused cost increases should not be allowed to upset the general stability of price and wage levels.

Apart from these special cases, do we have to use, even in a full program, across-the-board subsidies to all producers of a product, like the subsidies on meat and butter in World War II? The answer ought to be "No," and it could be "No," given a proper stabilization program from the beginning of the war and given an acceptable prewar balance of interests between groups, which was reflected in the wartime controls program. Across-the-board food subsidies were established in the United States in 1943 because they were considered the only practicable way to roll back rising food prices to a level that would make tight wage control feasible. Use of such subsidies—in wartime or in a defense period—is evidence of failure of both government and the interest groups to face the realities of the situation in the beginning and to get together on a sensible, effective stabilization program.[6]

6. This does not, of course, refer to the special cases of subsidies to take care of war-caused dislocations, treated in the preceding paragraph. The state-

6. *Preventing Shifts to Higher-Priced Items*

The average of prices charged consumers for a group of items may be raised markedly without an increase in the price of a single item, simply by a shift by producers from output of lower-priced to higher-priced items. All of us remember that low-priced clothing disappeared from the stores in the United States in World War II. Under the influence of strong demand many makers of women's dresses, men's and women's suits, men's shirts, children's clothing and other kinds of apparel discontinued their low-priced lines. In the absence of effective controls it is quite natural for producers to shift output from low- to high-priced lines, especially if their costs are rising. The higher-priced lines or models of many durable and nondurable goods normally carry higher profit margins.

Disappearance of lower-priced clothing accounted for the bulk of the increase of 23 per cent in retail clothing prices recorded by the Bureau of Labor Statistics between April 1943 and June 1946. The same thing happened in house furnishings and furniture. And those three fields—clothing, house furnishings and furniture—were the only major fields in the BLS consumers' price index in which the average of prices was not effectively stabilized over the two years between the summer of 1943 and the summer of 1945.[7]

Price ceilings in themselves cannot prevent shifts to production of higher-priced lines or models. One can imagine

---

ment in the text refers to the United States. In countries heavily dependent on food imports, such as England, extensive use of across-the-board subsidies on food may be unavoidable.

7. The consumers' price index reflected higher average prices in these fields because the next higher-priced items were brought into the index (or given a larger weight if they were already in the index) as lower-priced items disappeared from the stores.

that an omniscient price agency could rearrange profit margins on items in all price lines or ranges so that there would be no inducement to production shifts. Actually, no price agency will have the knowledge to do this or the time and manpower to acquire it. Furthermore, there would be great opposition by business to any such rearrangement of "normal" profit margins.

In practice, an effective program to prevent marked shifts from production of lower- to higher-priced lines or models must include a combination of (1) controls on materials to channel them into lower-priced items, or controls on facilities to ensure their normal use on these items[8] and (2) some price adjustments on lower-priced items.

When war requires that civilian consumption be cut to the bone it is wise to limit output of apparel to specified economy models that save materials and labor and can be sold at relatively low prices.

7. *Rationing of Consumer Goods*

Rationing of consumer goods is another basic element of a full stabilization program. When consumers cannot legally buy a product without ration tickets, excess demand can be cancelled by fitting the number of ration tickets to the available supply of the product—just as with allocation of industrial materials. Without rationing, price ceilings on most consumer goods would break down in the face of very large excess demand, and extensive black markets would develop.[9] The "breaking point" would vary depending on

8. For example, a "loom freeze" may require that looms continue to work on the same products (and same price lines) as before.

9. The points made in the last two sentences might suggest that rationing makes price ceilings unnecessary, as many, indeed, contend. This is discussed in the section on rationing in the next chapter.

the nature of the market. Where it is easy for new producers or middlemen to enter the field, black markets can develop quickly with only moderate excess demand. For example, meat animals can be bought by new slaughterers who sell to new (black-market) wholesalers, retailers, restaurants or night clubs. Additional examples such as poultry, fish, women's dresses, children's clothing and furniture readily suggest themselves.

In the case of cigarettes, new automobiles and tires, on the other hand, it is not easy for new manufacturers to get into the business and the producers of leading brands or makes seem to have substantial control over their distribution channels. In these circumstances price ceilings probably will hold quite well, without rationing, even when shortages are severe.[10]

In a future world war shortages of many consumer goods would probably be much greater than in World War II, because of larger cutbacks in civilian output. This would call for more rationing.[11] But rationing schemes are complex and costly both in dollars and manpower. At the height of its operation in World War II, OPA's expenditures on rationing seem to have been more than twice as much as those on price and rent control. Of about 60,000 paid OPA employees, approximately 35,000 were local board clerks, occupied principally with rationing.[12] Rationing should be confined to cases where it is clearly needed, especially in a limited defense program, to which we now turn.

10. We are speaking here of new cars and new tires. Black markets can easily develop in used cars and used tires.

11. Also, rationing has other purposes in addition to aiding price control. See Chapter 9.

12. H. C. Mansfield and Associates, *A Short History of OPA,* U. S. Government Printing Office, Washington, 1948, pp. 224-26.

A Limited Program for a Limited Defense

The preceding sketch of a full program of direct stabilization controls for all-out war or other serious emergency provides a kind of check list for discussing the controls needed in the defense period. These may approach a full program at times. But direct controls will probably not be needed part of the time, and a limited direct controls program should be sufficient much of the time.

Without effective controls the danger in the defense period is chronic inflation averaging 3 per cent or more a year, with larger doses in hump periods offsetting the years of little or no price rise. As a practical matter it is unlikely that the price level can be kept completely stable during a build-up. Adjustments in some prices and in some wage rates or other income rates will be needed for reasons of equity or to aid supply. In such periods there will be few offsetting reductions. Nor will the public want a stabilization program either as complete or as tight as in wartime. Probably the best we can hope to do is to hold price rises in build-up periods to 1, 2 or 3 per cent a year, and prevent any increases at other times. Even this will require real effort.

Adequate Fiscal and Credit Policies

In the defense period, fiscal policies should prevent the appearance of an inflationary gap—except, perhaps, during temporary peaks of defense expenditure—and the goal of credit policy should be to limit credit expansion to the rate of increase in the physical volume of the country's output.[13]

These fiscal and credit policies should prove feasible so

---

13. In Chapter 4 we saw that credit authorities will have to permit larger credit expansion than this if price and wage increases occur independently on a wide scale, especially if they are in defense industries.

long as the defense take does not ordinarily go above 25 per cent of total national production. *In this chapter we assume that such fiscal and credit policies will be maintained throughout the period of a limited defense program.* Clearly, repression of inflation by direct controls will not work long in the face of a wide, continuing inflationary gap. In a long defense period, to consider such repression an alternative to adequate fiscal and credit measures would be like advocating slow poisoning as a better way than diet to treat overweight.

Direct Controls to Curb Certain Pressures

Selective price ceilings to reinforce allocations or priorities, and more or less general price and wage controls to overcome panic buying, to repress inflation during a brief peak of defense spending, or to combat a price-wage spiral—these are the valid uses of price and wage controls, as we saw in Chapter 4.

Excess of government expenditure over cash intake creates inflationary pressure; and easy money—permitting individuals and businesses to borrow at least a large part of what they want to borrow—is inflationary. Both enable total spending to increase faster than total output. But there are also other kinds of inflationary pressure. The public's state of mind—what businessmen, workers, consumers and farmers think is going to happen to supplies of goods and to prices—has proved to be an important inflationary (or deflationary) force. At times it may have as much influence as the condition of the government budget and credit policy. Psychology plays a leading role in panic buying and in a price-wage spiral. Union politics and interunion rivalries also have a bearing on the spiral. Important too are the attitudes of business and of labor toward price and wage policies—

whether business managements and unions try to do what they can to prevent inflation, or try to "beat the game," or follow an in-between policy.

The term inflationary pressure, as used in the rest of this chapter, means inflationary pressure from people's psychology and attitudes on price and wage policies. To repeat, we are assuming here that fiscal and credit policies will in general prevent both an inflationary gap and an inflationary credit expansion.

The extent of inflationary pressure coming from the public state of mind and from attitudes toward price and wage policies obviously is not easy to determine. You cannot measure it with a gauge like steam pressure. Even the new electronic computing machines cannot calculate it, because there is no formula to use. Like many important things in life, it is a matter of judgment based on a careful look at facts and expressions of opinion.

Varying the Program with Changes in Pressure

Inflationary pressure from psychology and attitudes toward price and wage policies is likely to change with changes in the scale of the defense program. If the inflationary pressure appears and disappears, the problem is to turn the direct controls on and off. If the pressure varies from severe to moderate (or vice versa), the problem is to change from a fuller stabilization program with tight standards to a more limited program with less restrictive standards (or vice versa).

General inflationary pressure obviously disappears when a hump build-up is followed by a trough bringing general business recession.[14] Even though no recession occurs or is

14. We are here using the terms "build-up," "hump," and "trough," to

expected, it may also disappear when a hump is followed by enough of a drop so that inflationary psychology and attitudes become dormant.

After a build-up, defense expenditure might simply flatten out, instead of falling, and remain steady for several years. In that case inflationary pressure might subside immediately, especially if the public expected a drop, rather than another rise, a few years ahead. Or, it might not disappear right away, especially if another build-up seemed an imminent possibility. In this situation removal of price and wage controls would be taking chances with inflation and would place a heavy responsibility for voluntary restraint on business and labor.

After a few years, however, a constant dollar expenditure on defense would become a smaller percentage of the growing national output. Also, maintenance of stable prices for a time might discourage inflationary psychology, especially if the possibility of a new build-up faded. Hence unless new trouble came into the picture the direct controls probably could be removed with safety in a few years.

In the meantime, while direct controls were still needed, the flattening out of defense demand might ease inflationary pressure sufficiently to permit some moderation in the direct controls program.[15]

With a drop in defense demand to a plateau not far below its peak, inflationary pressure might continue for a time,

---

refer to changing levels of defense expenditure—the simplest indicator of change in the scale of the defense program.

15. Conceivably there might be instances where inflationary pressure would remain just as strong after the defense program flattened out or fell off, so that no moderation of the direct control program would be safe. It seems much more likely, however, that inflationary pressure would usually decline and the program could be moderated—especially if pressure had previously been severe and a fairly full program of direct controls had been in force.

although with less force. In this case, also, a shift to a more limited direct controls program would be appropriate.

How is it possible to determine changes in inflationary pressure coming from changes in states of mind and attitudes? As noted earlier, there is no formula for this. Judgments have to be based on the number of prices falling below ceilings and their behavior, changes in the number and kind of requests for increases in ceiling prices and for wage increases, statements by businessmen and union officials, conclusions of expert observers, study of public opinion, and the like. In the range between the two clear cases of general business recession and persistent, strong inflationary pressure judgments always will be fallible and we shall have to take some chances—one way or the other.

Fuller and More Limited Controls Programs

Any direct controls program must give an acceptable balance of interests among groups; and include some limitation on the use of price and wage increases as incentives and some absorption of cost increases—the first two in our list of seven principal elements.

It is as true in peacetime as in war that no government stabilization program will work unless it provides a balance of group interests. Unfortunately, to attain and keep such a balance may be even harder in peace than in war. With a possibility that direct controls may have to last somewhat longer and with patriotism nearer a peacetime normal, each group may be more fearful of sacrificing more than "its share." Furthermore, at times during the defense period some or all of the annual increase in national output can go into the civilian economy—into personal consumption, new private business capital for nondefense purposes, and nondefense government activities. If direct controls are in effect then, they will have to bring about a sharing of this added income acceptable to the various interest groups.

Obviously there can be no effective brakes on prices and wages if incentive increases are widespread, or if sellers are free to cover all cost increases fully in price advances; hence limitations on incentive increases and reasonable absorption of cost increases are indispensable to a direct controls program.

On the other hand, little if any rationing of consumer goods may be needed in the defense period. With the strong fiscal and credit controls that we are assuming, cases of large excess demand for consumer goods are likely to be confined chiefly to metal-using products the output of which has to be reduced in defense build-ups. Ceiling prices on the chief products in this class—automobiles, refrigerators, washing machines and the like—will work pretty well without rationing even with large excess demand, as we noted above.[16]

Whether or not any of the other four principal elements of a full program—restrictions on automatic escalator increases, differential pricing, subsidies, and prevention of shifts from lower-priced to higher-priced items—will be needed from time to time during the defense period will depend, of course, on the force of inflationary pressure. This holds also for the coverage of price ceilings, the types of ceilings and the strictness of price and wage standards.

Suppose there were a wave of panic buying, with no prospect of a price-wage spiral. That could probably be stopped by a prompt general freeze of prices and wages accompanied by severe limitations on the use of incentive price and wage

16. See p. 178. Again, the statement applies to new products, not used articles.

increases and substantial absorption of cost increases. Restrictions on automatic price and wage escalators would be helpful, but might not be necessary. The other principal elements —differential pricing, subsidies, prevention of production shifts from lower- to higher-priced items and rationing— probably would not be needed.

The Pressure of a Price-Wage Spiral

However, if a wave of panic buying is serious enough to call for general price and wage controls it will probably be accompanied by a potential spiral. A large and rapid defense build-up is likely to bring both.

With such a build-up, a spiral can be halted or prevented only with some restrictions on automatic price and wage increases. It may be necessary to suspend temporarily the provisions tying together wage rates and consumer prices, farm prices and other prices, and other common escalators, if we really want to curb the spiraling forces.

With a strong spiral under way or in the making it is important to hold down both the number and the extent of price increases. Differential pricing and subsidies for high-cost marginal supplies of key commodities can contribute to this. Pressure for wage increases may be moderated if retail stores continue to have the usual stocks of lower-priced clothing, house furnishings and consumer hard goods. Controls may be needed to ensure this. All these elements may not be required to curb inflation in every build-up, but we should be ready to use them if they are needed. Overcoming strong inflationary forces is always a hard job.

Most—perhaps all—the inflation of 1950 and 1951 after the Korean outbreak could have been prevented if stringent credit restrictions had been imposed in June or July, accompanied by a general freeze of prices and wages, temporary suspension of automatic escalators, limitations on incentive price and wage increases and the requirement of substantial absorption of cost increases. Together with the good fiscal policy we actually followed this would have constituted a strong program. The other four elements—differential pricing, subsidies, controls to preserve normal output of lower-priced items, and rationing—probably would not have been needed. Had this program been adopted, it might have been possible to moderate the direct stabilization controls after four to six months as the initial inflationary psychology subsided and it became clear that the spiral was being kept from getting under way.

When Pressure Lessens

A change from a fuller to a more limited direct controls program—reflecting the lessening of inflationary pressure—may involve removing controls from some parts of the economy, more use of loose formula price ceilings, and less restrictive price and wage standards. These will be treated in the next two chapters. Furthermore, most of the principal elements other than limitation on use of incentive price and wage increases and absorption of cost increases can probably be dropped as inflationary pressure declines. If direct price and wage controls are continued for a few years in a period of moderate inflationary pressure we would not want to restrict escalators that are desirable in normal times. Similarly, limitations on shifts of production should not be imposed at the cost of hobbling the introduction of new styles and varieties or preventing larger output in higher-priced lines or models in response to consumers' desires. Differential pricing and marginal subsidies to help hold down living costs will be needed as a rule only in a time of severe inflationary pressure. But marginal subsidies on basic materials that save the government money on munitions or other defense goods would be good business at any time.[17]

Do We Need a Two-Platoon System?

The legislative and administrative difficulties of turning direct controls on and off with emergence and disappearance of inflationary pressure were noted in Chapter 4. If the change from a limited to a more complete program required speedy enactment of legislation to give additional powers or appropriations, the same kind of difficulty would probably be met. This could be avoided in part if Congress would keep enabling legislation so broad that the program could be varied by administrative action to use as many or as few of the seven principal elements as seemed necessary and to shift standards from tight to less restrictive and vice versa.

The Defense Production Act, as amended in 1951 and 1952, seemed to give authority to make substantial use of all the seven principal elements, except subsidies, and to change the extent of their use. It authorized limited use of subsidies, where these were necessary to maintain high-cost supplies of domestic production of nonagricultural raw materials, and, in the form of government purchase and resale at a loss, under certain circumstances to obtain additional supplies of materials needed for defense.

17. This assumes, of course, that the subsidies are administered so that they encourage reduction of costs by all producers and curtail the amount of subsidy when nonsubsidized output can replace subsidized output. All producers, whether subsidized or not, should be permitted to retain a part of any economies they can make. If nonsubsidized output can be expanded to replace some subsidized output this should be done unless it is deemed wiser on grounds of national security to hold it in reserve. To get the desired result a subsidy must often be guaranteed for a period of a few years but it can be discontinued at the expiration of the specified term, if it is no longer needed.

The Act contained some important limitations on the authority to use these principal elements. An amendment in 1951 severely limited absorption of cost increases at wholesale and retail levels, requiring allowance of customary percentage markups. We have seen above that allowance of the usual percentage margins should be the general rule in the original establishment of ceiling prices at wholesale or retail, or in replacing an original freeze of prices. During severe inflationary pressure a reasonable absorption of cost increases out of these margins should complement absorption of cost increases by manufacturing industries. The amount of absorption that can be required on manufactured products also was limited somewhat by an amendment in 1951 providing for increases in ceiling prices to reflect all cost increases up to July 26, 1951. The amendment did not forbid reasonable absorption of subsequent cost increases.

An amendment in 1952 exempted from price control fresh and processed fruits and vegetables, important elements in the food budgets of most families.

In 1952, Congress also weakened the authority for credit control, by prohibiting use of restrictions on consumer-durable-goods credit, and requiring suspension of controls on residential real estate credit when the number of houses started in a three-month period exceeds an annual rate of 1.2 million.

Controls in Practice

In practice it will probably be hard for the control agencies themselves to vary their programs markedly. A staff that has been administering a fairly full program with tight standards is likely to find it difficult to shift over to a more limited program with looser standards. To many persons this will seem like compromising virtue, or giving in when the enemy is almost beaten. The change will be made more difficult if over the country many people fail to understand the wisdom of the policy of varying the program in rhythm with changes in inflationary pressure.

Perhaps to go in the opposite direction would be easier, but strengthening and tightening a program will also encounter difficulties. Additional personnel must be secured quickly. Those who have been administering loose controls must tighten them up and become "tougher" in their attitude. Many may not be able to do this. The very nature of the job probably operates a kind of natural selection of personnel according to attitude and conceptions of the task. Evidently the administration of direct stabilization controls that varied substantially from time to time would call for a kind of two-platoon system.

It would be undesirable to retain any longer than necessary a stringent direct controls program that puts severe curbs on the economic freedom of business, labor, and others, and on the flexibility of the market. Hence, should it prove impossible in practice to change from a fuller to a more limited direct controls program at a time when inflationary pressure from psychology and attitudes has declined substantially, it would probably be wiser to remove the controls entirely, except, perhaps, for selective price ceilings. But we should be sensible enough to prefer a relatively loose direct controls program to any substantial degree of inflation.

9. Price Control and Rationing

THE STRENGTH of direct stabilization controls will depend on the types of price ceilings, the coverage of price control and the pricing standards used, as well as the content of principal elements discussed in the preceding chapter. The sections on price control in the present chapter will consider types of ceilings, coverage and pricing standards with particular attention to differences between a fuller and a more limited program.

Types of Price Ceilings

There are three chief types of price ceilings: freeze ceilings, formula ceilings and dollar-and-cents ceilings.

Freeze Ceilings

A freeze ceiling says that the prices charged by a seller in a specified "base period" (usually a few days or weeks back) become the maximum legal prices unless or until adjustments are made by the price control agency. A broad freeze is obviously the only feasible means of preventing or checking with one stroke a broad inflationary movement. A price freeze can curb a price surge due to panic buying. A price and wage freeze together can prevent or halt a wage-price spiral.

However, a freeze is only a stopgap. In the first place, few know exactly what the legal ceiling prices are, which hampers both compliance and enforcement. Many do not remember exactly what they paid for pork loins or a box of crackers or a bunch of carrots a week or two ago. In the case

of things we buy only once in a while—such as shoes, refrigerators, medicines, razors—many will not have purchased the articles in question in the base period. Moreover, many small sellers, and some others, do not keep detailed records of their prices, even a few weeks back, and
will not remember exactly what they were charging on many
items.

Of course business buyers are more likely to have records
of the prices they paid in the base period. But where the regulation freezes "the highest price charged by the seller in
the base period to a purchaser in the same class" no buyer
can know whether the price he paid was "the highest price"
or not.

Second, whenever a seller can change the style or composition of an article, making it a "new good," it is not this
product's price which was frozen, and the seller thus escapes
the freeze. Such a change will take quite a time in the case
of complex products of mass production, such as automobiles and other large durables, especially where manufacturers are accustomed to bring out new models only once a
year. But for many items of apparel and housewares—for
example, women's dresses, men's shirts, curtains, mops, water
glasses—change in style or composition can be made in a
few weeks, or even over the week-end.

Third, at any given time there are always some inequities
in the existing price structure. When these are frozen into legal ceilings there must be provision for adjustments. A typical example involves both wholesale and retail prices. Many
retailers set their prices by applying a fixed markup to what
they pay for the goods. After a rise in wholesale prices many
retailers will not immediately raise their prices because they
are selling goods purchased earlier at a lower cost. A freeze

catches these retailers "with their prices down," and they will suffer a squeeze as they replenish their inventories unless their ceiling prices are raised or the ceilings of their suppliers lowered. The second alternative is seldom practicable, however, because it would call for lowering ceilings at the manufacturing level, which might in turn require a rollback of prices of materials or wage rates.

Prices set by long-term contracts or by custom are also a field where some inequities will be "frozen in." House rents are an obvious example.

Formula Ceilings

A formula ceiling is a maximum price computed according to a formula specified in a regulation. The calculation of the ceiling price may be left to the seller or made by the price agency on the basis of information supplied by the seller.

This type of ceiling applies in several kinds of cases. One is that of products made to special order or specification, such as special alloys, chemical compounds and many machine tools. In this case, formulas often provide for adding to specified elements of cost (such as labor and materials) a margin for other costs and profit.

Another is that of new styles or varieties of a product. The purpose of pricing formulas here is to keep ceilings in line with the ceilings on the old styles and varieties. This is especially important when tight materials or manpower make it undesirable to use either in developing new goods. It is also important when a shift to new goods simply to escape firm price control would raise living costs. In these situations formulas for ceilings for "new goods" must ensure profit margins on the new goods no greater than those on the old styles and varieties. In practice, this is very difficult to accomplish.

When producers are permitted to calculate their ceiling prices by applying a specified formula the resulting ceilings will usually be higher than if the computations are made by the price control agency. In most cases, application of formulas involves a considerable amount of interpretation and judgment, leaving room to give one's self the benefit of the doubt. Nevertheless, much of the work of calculating formula ceilings must be left to producers because it is so costly in manpower and time. Outright violations, however, can be discouraged by sample spot checks, as is done with income tax returns.

A simple kind of formula ceiling, often called "margin control," is especially useful in wholesale and retail trades where the customary pricing practice is to add to the purchase cost of the goods a customary margin or markup. Understanding of price ceilings and compliance with them by wholesalers and retailers is greatly promoted by use of customary pricing formulas in regulations applying to them. This is especially true with small wholesalers and retailers.

Formulas are also useful in making a broad realignment of price relations. The application of general price control on January 26, 1951 froze prices at levels of the preceding five weeks. Prices of manufactured goods had risen very unevenly between the Korean outbreak in June 1950 and the December-January base period for the freeze.

To correct the disparities the Office of Price Stabilization issued a formula regulation in the spring of 1951 designed to put ceilings of different manufactured products on roughly the same basis in relation to their pre-Korean costs. This formula provided for calculation of new ceiling prices, to replace the freeze by adding to pre-Korean prices the increases in labor and material costs between July 1, 1950 and specified dates in the spring of 1951. The cutoff date for labor increases was March 15; for materials the cutoff dates varied. This formula was in effect replaced by an amendment to the Defense Production Act in 1951, providing for recalculation of ceilings by adding cost increases of all kinds up to July 26, 1951.

With formula ceilings, as with freeze ceilings, buyers do not know what the legal maximum prices are, unless sellers are required to state them in dollars and cents.

Dollar-and-Cents Ceilings

Dollar-and-cents ceilings are maximum prices so stated in the regulation establishing them, or by a poster or other public notice. Obviously dollar-and-cents ceilings are the best from the standpoint of compliance and enforcement because, in general, everyone knows what the ceilings are.[1]

The scope of dollar-and-cents ceilings is not limited to those worked out directly by the price agency from data on prevailing prices or by the application of a formula. A seller subject to a freeze or formula ceiling can be required to post his ceiling prices in dollars and cents in his place of business, or to mark them on the articles or on attached tags or tickets or to give some other form of notice to his customers. A device called "preticketing" can be used to tell both the retailer and the consumer the retail ceiling price of an article. Preticketing works like this: the manufacturer of a handbag or a shirt computes the retail ceiling price by adding to his own

1. This is not literally true in every case. Where differences in grade, quality or quantity are not easy to determine you may not know whether or not you are getting the same article even though you know the ceiling price. A box of candy may contain fewer pieces. When the ingredients of a can of soup are changed the can will look the same and the soup may taste about the same even though the nutritive value may have been lowered.

ceiling price distributive margins for wholesalers and retailers specified by the price control agency. He then marks
this retail price on a ticket or tag which must remain attached to the shirt or handbag until it is sold to the ultimate
consumer.

A tight price control program for severe inflationary pressure calls for wide use of dollar-and-cents ceilings and calculation of formula ceilings—where they are used—by the price
agency for commodities important in living or business costs.
In periods of moderate inflationary pressure these are not
necessary on so extensive a scale.

Coverage of Price Control

In full war, price control must cover practically everything,
with ceilings even on less essential goods and on nonessential
goods if any are left in production. Otherwise large profits
on them may attract manpower and materials from more important uses and interfere with controls designed to direct
these resources to the fields where they are most needed. Furthermore, for the sake of high morale producers of essential
goods must not have reason to feel that the less a product
is needed the looser the control and the larger the profits
on it.

Coverage in the Defense Period

In the defense period there may be times when "selective"
price control is sufficient—that is, ceilings on particular commodities in short supply. The purpose may be to aid allocation or priority controls or to forestall the start of a spiral
in commodity areas, particularly minerals and metals, which
feel the first heavy impact of a build-up of defense demand.

To prevent or halt a general surge of panic buying, or a

price and wage spiral already moving, or threatening to move, across the economy, price control must be quite extensive. But it need not cover everything.

Certain Exemptions

Sales by very small manufacturers, wholesalers and retailers (including service establishments) can be exempted, except in the case of basic food items or other goods especially important in living costs or business costs. Exemptions can also be made for products of little or no significance in living costs[2] or business costs. When we get beyond the long list of obvious things—*objets d'art,* stuffed animals, hors d'oevres, fancy buttons, experimental apparatus and the like —drawing the line as to where price increases will not feed the buying spree or the spiral is a matter of judgment.

It is probably safe also to exempt luxury goods and the highest-priced lines of apparel, furniture, house furnishings and the like, provided effective steps are taken, if they are needed, to prevent substantial shifts of production from lower-priced lines to these. Stiff excise taxes on luxury goods and higher-priced lines would be sound fiscal policy and would also help check any tendency to increase their output at the expense of lower- and medium-priced goods.[3] This exemption policy should not apply, however, to automobiles and other products using the scarcer materials and manpower needed in defense production. Output of these will

2. This does not mean, of course, that all commodities not included in the consumers' price index can be exempted. That index is composed of a sample of commodities believed to be representative of most goods and services bought by moderate-income families in large cities. Since the commodities in the index are only a *sample,* many important things are omitted.

3. The British did this in World War II with their so-called purchase tax. The suggestion in the text is similar to that of J. K. Galbraith in *Hearings before the Joint Committee on the Economic Report,* 82d Cong., 1st sess., p. 355.

have to be cut back substantially in a defense build-up. With the resulting shortages stabilization controls should do nothing that might encourage a shift to the production of a larger proportion of the higher-priced models; nor should it discourage a shift in the opposite direction that would produce a larger number of units.

Commodities Difficult to Control

There are many commodities for which effective ceiling price control is very difficult because of characteristics of the commodity or the market. We have noted this problem in regard to many kinds of clothing, house furnishings and so on, where the product can be changed all too easily and quickly.

Great difficulties also exist wherever a commodity is sold by a large number of firms, for example, grains and many other farm products, cattle, hogs, poultry, fish, women's dresses and underwear, children's apparel, scrap metals and other waste materials. In these markets prices rise and fall quickly in response to changes in demand. The individual seller cannot set or "administer" his price as can the large producers of automobiles, electrical equipment, aluminum, cigarettes and many other goods. He is accustomed to follow the price swings normal in his kind of market—to adhere to a steady ceiling price in the face of rising demand is outside his experience. Moreover, entry to this kind of market is usually easy for new producers, processors and middlemen. Hence black markets can develop quickly and are hard to police.

Another obstacle to effective price control in such markets is simply the difficulty of communicating with a great number of sellers, most of them small businessmen, in order to explain the provisions of the regulations and the reasons for them. In the case of agricultural products the possibility of direct sales from farmers to consumers presents additional difficulties.

Some hold that in a limited defense program we should not attempt price control in markets like this or on commodities where the product can easily be varied. Were this advice followed it would mean exemption of food and clothing items comprising a substantial part of our living costs; also exemption of scrap metals which are important in munitions production. Commodities in these areas of special difficulty that are unimportant in living or business costs should be exempt from price control. But exemption of the others when inflationary pressure is strong would threaten stabilization.

Price Control of Basic Cost-of-Living Items

High personal income taxes plus tight credit to curb increases in demand for these and other commodities are indispensable, as we saw in Chapter 4. But, as we also saw in that chapter, these measures cannot deal successfully with sudden buying surges, or with increases on individual commodities, though these increases help stimulate a price-wage spiral. Price control on basic cost-of-living items is necessary both to strengthen control of living costs and to make wage control feasible. It would be hard, indeed, to convince workers that ceilings on meat, dresses, children's clothing and other cost-of-living items were not needed, so long as their wages were held down by direct control and their income taxes raised high enough. Price ceilings on many farm products including grains and fresh fruits and vegetables can usually be made effective enough to be worthwhile even though they have shortcomings.[4]

Moreover, in most of the food and clothing fields, effective control of processing margins between materials and end products is possible, and this in itself is worth something. Examples are meat, canned fruits and vegetables, men's suits and shirts, and work clothing. In many clothing items the cost of the raw material—cotton, rayon or wool—is in fact not a large element in total cost. Furthermore, human ingenuity probably can devise more effective ways to cope with obstacles to effective price control of food and clothing.

With a decline in inflationary pressure and a change from fuller to more limited direct controls, price control might be removed in some cases presenting major technical difficulties. If substantial inflationary pressure remains quite general, however, it is probably wiser to change the types of ceilings, the pricing standards and the number of the principal elements used, than to decontrol extensively.

There are two reasons for this. In practice, wage control must be general rather than selective, and general wage control scarcely could be maintained unless price control covered most of the area of inflationary pressure. Second, an inflationary spiral can start almost anywhere and does not always "telegraph" its point of origin.

Decontrol When Prices Fall below Ceilings?

The problem of partial decontrol probably will come up in another way. With a decline in general inflationary pres-

4. It is often difficult to design workable ceilings that apply to sales at the farm or to local handlers of farm products. But ceilings can take hold as the farm products come into regional or national markets or go to processors or, in the case of fresh produce, to wholesalers or retailers.

sure from severe to moderate, some prices—and perhaps many—will fall below ceilings. In the latter part of 1951 and early 1952, many soft-goods prices, along with some others, were below ceilings. When this happens common sense seems to say, "Remove those ceilings—they are not needed now." If inflationary pressure is likely to disappear in most segments of the economy, then removal of those ceilings would be an appropriate way to begin general decontrol. But decontrol when prices fall below ceilings would not be wise, given a strong possibility that these prices soon would rise again because of special factors in their demand-supply relations or a general surge of inflationary pressure. So long as general wage control is needed, it would be ill-advised to take a ponderable chance of increased living costs through partial removal of price ceilings.

There has been much discussion of the relative merits of suspension of ceiling price regulations as against outright removal. Suspension means that the applicability of a regulation is lifted for a specified period or until further notice, while it remains on the books ready to go into force on notice by the administrator. (Obviously, suspension may relate to specified provisions, regulation or the whole.)

Removal of regulations should occur only when it seems safe to discard general price and wage controls, whether or not selective ceilings are to be retained. Suspension of ceilings is appropriate where particular prices have fallen below them, even though general inflationary pressure continues and general price and wage control cannot yet be revoked. Suspensions of individual ceilings also are appropriate when it is impossible to determine whether or not substantial general inflationary pressure has ceased.

Some may ask, "What is the point of suspension? If prices are below ceilings, the ceiling is not in operation." But regulations usually require sellers to keep certain records, to file prices of new products, to attach tickets to articles showing the retail ceiling price, or to do other things requiring extra work. Sellers should be relieved of this burden as soon as these procedures are not needed.

Suspension, instead of removal, indicates to the public that although inflationary pressure has eased in spots, in general it has not disappeared, and it may return even in those places.

In the first half of 1952, inflationary pressure had greatly diminished and the question arose whether price and wage controls could be removed. However, consumer prices were still edging up, many wage rates were rising, and defense expenditures were scheduled to increase. The issue was whether the chances of a resurgence of inflationary forces in 1952 or 1953 were sufficient to call for retention of the apparatus of general direct controls (with or without many suspensions) and extension of the statutory authority. The Office of Price Stabilization followed a policy of caution and used suspension instead of removal. Whether or not a shift from general to selective price control would have been safe in the spring or summer of 1952, it appears that OPS would have been safe in applying its suspension policy sooner and more widely.

In June 1952, Congress extended for ten months (to April 30, 1953) the statutory authority for general price and wage controls included in the Defense Production Act. A policy declaration included in amendments to the Act, passed in June, called for termination of general control of prices and wages as soon as possible, consistent with the purposes and policies of the Act, and in the meantime, suspensions along lines similar to those sketched above.

Differences in Costs

If prices drop below ceilings because costs have been reduced, should ceiling prices be lowered or removed? Suppose that direct controls are maintained for four or five years because general inflationary pressure continues strong enough to produce a surging spiral without them. This might be the case, for example, on a gradually rising plateau of defense expenditure even with the budget continuously in balance. Over the years, prices of some products might decline substantially, not because of surplus supplies or a drop in demand, but because of reductions in unit costs. In a normal peacetime economy with a generally stable price level prices of some commodities decline over a period of years, and prices of other commodities rise, reflecting differences in cost movements.

But if we have to maintain general direct controls over a period long enough for marked differences in cost movements between industries, should the direct controls be so administered as to bring results approaching as closely as possible those of normal times? This is a debatable question. It is not always easy to distinguish between permanent and temporary cost reductions. We do not want to discourage initiative in lowering costs by making ceilings chase down on the heels of costs. This might result in higher future prices than would the decontrol of these commodities. But a middle course is certainly both possible and preferable, at least for manufacturing or processing industries. This is to reduce ceilings at a lag of six months to a year after cost reductions and on a standard that permits business to retain a substantial part of the economies.[5]

This policy would, of course, be difficult—perhaps impossible—to apply to imports such as wool, coffee and hides, and to domestic farm products the prices of which fluctuate markedly in response to changes in demand.

Pricing Standards

Pricing standards are needed for setting original ceilings (except by freeze) and for making adjustments to the original ceilings for an industry as a whole or for individual firms. There must also be standards for ceilings for new goods, for new sellers, and for special cases of various kinds. A long book could be written on pricing standards. Here we deal briefly only with the crucial problem of standards for industry-wide increases in ceilings.

Standards for such increases have a twofold purpose: (1) to provide for adjustments where they are required on grounds of equity or to help secure needed supplies; (2) to set limits to the amounts of the price adjustments so they do not exceed requirements for these purposes.

When inflationary pressure is severe, standards for price increases must be tight. But given only moderate inflationary pressure, standards can and should be less restrictive, so they do not hinder such normal and desirable changes as relative differences in growth rates among industries, firms, products and regions to reflect changes in consumer preferences, in costs or in regional development.

---

5. Where it is clear that cost has fallen by a substantial amount merely because of a drop in the price of materials or purchased services, rather than because of economies introduced by managements, there would seem to be no reason against an immediate reduction in the ceiling price of the product— unless it appeared that the declines in cost were likely to be temporary.

Industry Earnings Standards

In Chapter 8 we saw that reasonable absorption of cost increases is one of the fundamental elements of effective price control. This calls for an earnings or profits standard by which to determine when an industry, having absorbed enough, is entitled to an increase in its ceiling prices.

There is a widely held view that price control should not involve any so-called "profit control." This is nonsense. It is impossible to put any limitation on price increases without keeping profits somewhat below what they otherwise would be. It is important, however, to make sure that price control does not cut profits below minimum desirable levels. Price control should not (and in practice could not) fix the exact amount of profit for each industry, let alone each firm, and then so manipulate ceilings as to allow no more and no less. But, to repeat, price control inevitably affects profits, and an earnings standard is necessary to ensure equitable treatment among industries in permitting or denying increases in ceiling prices.[6]

Kinds and Requirements of Earnings Standards

A satisfactory industry earnings standard may be in terms of percentage return on net worth (the capital investment of the owners), or percentage return on sales. In World War

6. Cf. the discussion "Price Control and Profit Control" in the *Capital Goods Review,* Machinery and Allied Products Institute, August 1951.

"For some reason the view is widely held, not least in Congressional circles, that price control should *not* involve profit control. It is not uncommon, therefore, for price administrators to be catechized by legislative committees as to their orthodoxy on this point of doctrine, and woe to the hapless official whose affirmation of faith lacks resonance and conviction. . . . (p. 1).

"If price control really becomes a combination of price and profit control when ceiling prices are adjusted by reference to a profits standard, there may be advantages in an honest recognition of the fact. There should be, indeed, substantial advantages. For if it is acknowledged by the price administrators

II, OPA used the average return on net worth of each industry in the prewar years 1936-1939 as the general standard for minimum reasonable earnings of an industry in wartime. Under a directive of the Economic Stabilization Administrator OPS used the standard of 85 per cent of the return on net worth in the best three years of the four-year period 1946-1949. In both cases these were standards set by Congress for the corporate excess profits tax. In both the price agency made exceptions when the base period earnings of a particular industry were considered abnormal. For example, OPS announced in February 1952 that a minimum return of 10 per cent on net worth was to be used as a guide in cases where industry earnings in the base period 1946-1949 were unreasonably low.

If an industry can expand sales volume without a proportionate increase in its net worth then an earnings standard in terms of return on net worth will give tighter price control than one in terms of return on sales. Suppose an industry's profits in the base period yielded an average return of 20 per cent on its net worth and 10 per cent on its sales; suppose further that sales grew by a third, without any increase in net worth, but that total dollar earnings rose by only a fifth, owing to absorption of some cost increases. Then return on net worth would have risen to 24 per cent while return on sales fell to 9 per cent. If the base period return on net worth was the standard, the industry would get

---

that they are in the business of profit control there is a chance that they will do a better job of it than if the pretense is maintained that nothing of the kind is going on.

"With such a frank acknowledgment of the facts, it will become apparent at once that there can be only one acceptable standard for the application of the profits test. *Industry price adjustments should be granted whenever the industry as a whole is making less than a fair and reasonable profit, the adjustment being calculated to restore such a profit. . . .*" (p. 3). Italics supplied.

no increase in its ceiling prices. If the standard was return on sales, an increase in ceiling prices would be due.[7]

An earnings standard in terms of a return on net worth is appropriate for a period of severe inflationary pressure. A return-on-sales standard would be better for a more limited stabilization program in a period of moderate inflationary pressure, especially if direct controls must be retained for several years.[8]

Whichever earnings standard is used it must be stated in terms of profits *before* income and excess profits taxes. If price ceilings in general were so raised as to preserve profits *after* income and excess profits taxes, profit receivers would escape profits tax increases designed to help pay the costs of war or of a defense program. However, the resulting price increases would raise the costs of war or defense, which in turn would call for further increases in tax rates, and so on around and around a vicious circle. If prices were raised to maintain business profits *after* taxes, then equal treatment of wage and salary workers would mean raising pay rates to maintain wage and salary incomes *after* personal income taxes. But to think of raising all prices, wage rates and other income rates in an attempt to preserve all incomes on an after-tax basis is to discuss a never-never land of finance.

7. Illustrative figures are as follows:

	Base Period	Now
Earnings	$10 million	$12 million
Sales	100 "	133.3 "
Net worth	50 "	50 "
Return on sales	10 per cent	9 per cent
Return on net worth	20 " "	24 " "

8. As a stimulus to efficiency it might be advisable to apply the return-on-net-worth standard to an industry that generally was not securing the normal, average increase in man-hour productivity (about 2.5 per cent a year), with a change to the return-on-sales standard when its productivity increase came up to this norm.

That objective cannot be attained in the world of reality. Money incomes after taxes could, indeed, be maintained; but only by inflating living and business costs and thereby cutting the real buying power of those money incomes.

Product Standards

The industry earnings standard is a basis for judging the general fairness of an industry's ceiling prices on all its products or on a broad group of products. Most industries sell more than one product or group of products. Hence there must also be a minimum standard for upward adjustment of ceiling prices for a single product or product line. A tight product standard would not exceed the average total cost of production of the industry for that product.[9]

A less restrictive standard would be total cost, plus some margin of profit.

The industry earnings standards and product standards described above are applicable to mining, manufacturing or processing industries and to some service industries. In many distributive trades an earnings standard in terms of net worth is not workable because of inadequate data on net worth. This is especially true of small sellers. The average percentage return on sales is usually available and this can be used for distributive trades. A product standard that fits the accounting practices of the distributive trades can be developed in terms of a trade's average "expense ratio" or the cost of doing business in a base period. This would become the lowest reasonable margin to be added to the cost of the

9. Considerations of fairness alone justify an even tighter standard, such as average manufacturing cost used by OPA in World War II, so long as over-all profits on all operations exceed a reasonable minimum. But, as OPA found out, there are great practical difficulties in applying a standard that seems to many to run counter to good business principles.

goods to the distributors, to arrive at the ceiling on a particular product or line of product.

The industry earnings standards and product standards here described are standards for *increases* in ceiling prices on grounds of equity. They are *not* standards for reducing ceiling prices that are above these minimum equitable levels.

Removal of Price Disparities

The earnings standard and product standard are bases for adjusting ceiling prices upward to maintain reasonable results. They are akin to standards for wage adjustment to remove inequities. If the disparities and distortions of an original freeze are very extensive, because the freeze was not imposed until some time after the impacts of a defense build-up began to make themselves felt, or after a spiral of inflation was well under way, an over-all readjustment of ceiling prices would be desirable to bring them back so far as possible to the relationships of a normal period.

In the case of manufactured products this can be done by recomputing all ceiling prices, adding to the prices of a pre-freeze normal period subsequent increases in cost up to a cutoff date. For such standardized commodities as graded lumber and the regular shapes and alloys of metals, this would be done on an industry-wide basis. For custom or style goods—automobiles, hats, furniture, for example—it would be done on an individual firm basis. The question of what kinds of cost increases to use presents difficult technical problems, unless the formula is limited to increases in direct factory labor and materials costs.[10]

10. The addition of increases in any or all overhead costs, for the purpose of realigning prices, is not bad in principle, but is almost impossible to apply well in practice. Many firms lack adequate cost accounting systems; cost accountants differ on methods of allocating general overhead expense among

Supply Cases

The pricing standards we have just been talking about are standards of fair treatment. Often they will also afford adequate incentives to furnish all the needed supply of a product. There will be instances, however, in which special adjustments, beyond any permitted by the earnings standard and the product standard, will be required to help overcome shortages of defense essentials or to remove price disparities leading to abnormally low output of some civilian goods. As with wage adjustments for manpower reasons, treated in the next chapter, it is hard to develop appropriate standards for these "supply" adjustments except on a case-by-case basis.

For a tight supply standard the general principle is to allow the smallest price increase that will do the job along with all practicable measures of control over the use of materials and facilities. Supply adjustments can often be confined to the particular producers who actually need them by means of individual company adjustments or other forms of differential pricing.

Farm Products

Special pricing standards are required for farm products. Neither cost of production nor rate of return on net worth (or any other measure of investment) apply to farm products, for the simple reason that the required data are not available. An industry earnings standard and a product standard can be applied to processors, but they cannot be used to set or adjust ceiling prices received by farmers them-

different products. The amendment to the Defense Production Act of 1951 providing for recalculation of ceilings by adding *all* cost increases up to July 26, 1951 is difficult, to say the least, to apply.

selves. In some instances, these standards are also not applicable to the first handlers of farm products.

Parity between the prices received by farmers and the prices they pay for the things they buy has been used for nearly two decades in standards for government support of farm prices. The purpose is to keep farm prices moving up more or less in step with the average of prices of what farmers buy—farm machinery, automobiles, clothing, coffee, sugar, for example—and to see that they do not fall unless prices of what they buy are also falling. The parity concept has been extended to ceiling price control, both in World War II and in the present defense period.

The desirability of using parity as a pricing standard for ceilings on farm products turns principally on two considerations: (1) whether or not parity is a desirable standard for farm prices in normal peacetime; (2) the criteria for calculating parity prices.

If parity is generally accepted as an appropriate standard to govern the behavior of farm prices in normal peacetime, then its use should be desirable, in principle, at least, in the defense period. As emphasized throughout this book we want to preserve so far as practicable all our basic values and institutions during the defense period.

The actual results of applying the parity principle can be quite different, however, depending on what goes into the calculations. This is a highly complex subject on which we cannot embark here. Suffice it to say that the emergency or semiemergency conditions of a defense program should not be exploited to make inflationary revisions of parity calculations. If any revisions are made they should be rather in the direction of getting parity prices of individual farm products more nearly into relationships that will encourage the desirable relative supplies of the various products—grains, fibers, fruits, vegetables, livestock and so on.

If the parity standard is used to adjust farm ceiling prices, the ceilings will rise with increases in prices of the things farmers buy. In a time of severe inflationary pressure, which calls for a hold-the-line policy everywhere, this automatic escalator should be suspended along with other automatic escalators, such as cost-of-living adjustments in wage rates and wage-rate adjustments to reflect increased productivity. If the anti-inflation program is successful, farm prices will not get much, if at all, out of line, even though the parity escalator is temporarily suspended, and they can be readjusted later when general inflationary pressure has disappeared.

The Importance of Price Relationships

Changes in relative prices are much more important in the farm field as a governor of what is produced than in industrial markets characterized by prices that are more or less administered. Farmers who grow corn can sell it or feed it to hogs. The relationship between the price of hogs and the price of corn is the deciding factor. Hence if a ceiling price is put on corn it must be geared to the ceiling price on hogs—and to ceiling prices on other feed grains as well. Indeed, with a severe feed grain shortage it is questionable whether effective ceilings on these products are possible. Given, for example, a corn price ceiling and an acute feed shortage, buyers can scarcely attract corn off farms where it can be fed to hogs, unless ceiling prices on hogs are greatly reduced.

This illustration is only one of many such situations in agriculture. Unless ceilings on farm products are carefully related to one another, there will be distortions in relative outputs of different farm products. The use of parity prices of individual commodities as their ceiling prices will bring about such distortions. In other words, parity does not establish a set of price relations that will stimulate production of the various commodities in the proportions that will best meet the demands of consumers—at these prices—plus the defense demands of government.

The fundamental reason for this is that the parity prices of individual farm products, being based to a large extent on their relative prices in a period long past (usually 1910-1914), are out of line with relative costs today. For example, economies in production of wheat and other crops have been much greater in the past few decades than in livestock. Thus maintenance of parity prices on these commodities would discourage output of livestock and stimulate the growing of wheat and other crops.

A new standard for parity calculation established by the Agricultural Act of 1948 attempted to correct in part this defect of the old formula by taking into account the relative prices of farm products in the most recent ten-year period. The Agricultural Act of 1949, however, nullified much of this change by providing that the old formula was to be used wherever it gave a higher parity price.

To avoid supply distortions, the relations between prices of individual farm products must be changed from those set by the parity standard. If the law requires (as it has) that no ceiling price for an individual farm product may be less than its parity price, it follows that such changes in price relations must be accomplished by raising ceiling prices of some commodities above their parity prices, or—what comes to the same thing—by incentive payments from government to producers of these commodities to raise their receipts above the revenue from sales at the ceiling prices.[11]

Supply distortions could also be removed in part by a change in the law to permit the parity principle to be applied to a group of related products as a whole. This would allow lower-than-parity ceilings on some products in the group (within a prescribed limit) when ceilings on others were above their parities, thus keeping the total for the whole group up to the parity standard. This would permit reconciliation of the parity principle with price relations needed for supply reasons (within a product group) and also hold inflation or subsidy down.

House Rents

Effective control of the rents of dwelling places is a very important part of direct stabilization controls to curb a price-wage spiral because rent is so substantial a part of living costs. In the case of rents, a freeze is singularly effective. Every tenant knows what rent he has been paying. Also, it is not easy to change the "product" to obtain a more lucrative ceiling price. Of course, upward adjustments in rents usually are permitted for improvements in the property or service. Such adjustments involve considerable additional expenditure by landlords, and a closer rein can be kept on them than on new-goods pricing in clothing and house furnishings. On the other hand, it seems to be fairly easy to reduce some items of operating expense, such as redecorating, repairs and maintenance—in other words, to change the

11. Such incentive payments could take different forms. The government might make subsidy payments direct to farmers, or to processors or other buyers who are expected to hand them on to farmers as supplements to the ceiling prices. Or the government could stand ready to buy any or all of the supply of a commodity and pay a supplement to the ceiling price on whatever it purchased.

"product" in the other direction to help "live within the ceiling."[12]

A rent freeze will involve some inequities just as will a price freeze or a wage freeze. Adjustment to remove these is chiefly a matter of getting out-of-line rents into line with prevailing ceilings for comparable facilities, including adjustments for rents frozen substantially below the current level. Landlords also must have reasonable compensation for improvements wanted by tenants and relief of genuine hardship. Formulation of standards for these various adjustments requires special technical knowledge of rental housing. A return-on-investment standard does not seem workable here, because comparable, reasonable estimates of investment in individual properties are not obtainable.

Experience shows that rent controls have often been the last of the government direct controls to be removed and have sometimes been kept for many years after other controls were lifted. This may be unfair to landlords in comparison with other businessmen, labor and farmers. It might also mean that in a fresh emergency another general freeze would perpetuate an inequity because, although the prices or income rates of other groups would be frozen at levels established in a period of no controls, rents would continue (except for specific adjustments here and there) at figures originally set many years earlier.

12. This is suggested by accounting studies by OPA of revenues and costs for samples of apartment houses and small structures in a number of cities for the years 1939-1945. In this period operating expense, exclusive of interest and depreciation, increased only about 4 per cent for the apartment house sample and declined about 7 per cent for the sample of small structures. Declines in expenditures for decorating, repairs, and maintenance were chief factors in the behavior of operating expenses. Between 1939 and 1945 gross revenues for the two samples increased about 13 and 14 per cent respectively, with the result of increases in net operating income of about 30 and 46 per cent respectively. See Harvey C. Mansfield and Associates, *A Short History of OPA*, U. S. Government Printing Office, Washington, 1948, pp. 138-39.

Rationing

Where there is a demand for a consumer good or a family of goods far beyond supplies, and new producers or middlemen can easily "get into the act," rationing can curtail consumer demand and thus greatly help make price ceilings effective. In the preceding chapter, it was suggested that we probably could get along without consumer rationing during a limited defense program, given the right fiscal and credit policies. Fiscal and credit policies are important because a wide inflationary gap and easy credit would create excess demand for nearly everything, and direct price and wage controls would work only with extensive rationing of consumer goods.

In war, rationing would be needed for three other purposes:

1. To ensure fair distribution of essential commodities in cases of severe shortages.

2. To aid effective prosecution of the war by making scarce goods indispensable to health, essential transportation and the like go where they will do the most good. (Examples in World War II were provision of tires and gasoline to doctors, workers in key jobs and trucking firms transporting army supplies.)

3. To help make production limitation orders and materials conservation orders effective by curtailing legal consumer demand for specified consumer goods to the volumes permitted by those orders.

Consumer goods rationing might be needed occasionally in the defense period for one or more of these purposes.

Coverage

In World War II, consumer goods rationing in the United

States covered a large part of the food field—meats, butter, fats, oils, canned fruits and vegetables, sugar and coffee—but was not applied to many other commodities. The principal commodities outside the food field to be rationed were automobiles, tires, gasoline, fuel oils, stoves, shoes, bicycles and typewriters. Supplies of many consumer goods increased enough to prevent severe shortages. It is estimated that the total volume of civilian consumption (real consumption, not dollar expenditure) grew in the war years to the following percentages of the 1939 level:[13]

> 1941 — 113 per cent
> 1942 — 112 " "
> 1943 — 116 " "
> 1944 — 120 " "
> 1945 — 128 " "

By the end of the war it was evidently about 25 per cent above 1939.

Severe shortages of consumer items were limited to a relatively few cases, such as sugar and tires, where supplies were cut drastically by a drop in imports; petroleum products where the military "take" was enormous; automobiles and typewriters, the manufacturing facilities for which were needed for munitions production; and meat, for which civilian demand increased tremendously with the growth in personal and family incomes.

Mobilization for total war in a period of full or almost

---

13. These percentage increases are computed from estimates of total personal consumption expenditures, *in 1939 dollars,* by the National Income Division of the Department of Commerce. See *National Income,* 1951 edition, p. 146. The Commerce estimates were made by deflating current dollar consumption expenditures in the various categories by specific price indexes constructed for each of these categories. See pp. 143-44. There is some error in estimates of this kind, but it seems clear that there was a substantial increase in total real consumption.

full employment would require much more extensive consumer rationing for each of the four purposes stated above.
Total consumption would have to be cut drastically. Consumption of many items would have to be reduced far
below the average for all consumption. Price ceilings and
limitation and conservation orders would have to have a lot
of help from rationing to make them effective.

In a limited defense program, given strong fiscal and
credit measures, acute shortages of consumer goods lasting
for a year or more may be limited chiefly to metal-using durable goods. For the more expensive products in this field
such as automobiles, refrigerators and television sets, limitations on installment credit can effectively curb consumer demand. True, the results will probably not be as equitable as
with a good rationing program. But if it is only a matter of
a year or two or three, if the shortages are not too severe and
if consumer stocks are high at the beginning (as they were
in 1950 and 1951 in autos and many other things), it seems
wiser to avoid rationing with its great expenditure of manpower and time.

Is it likely that rationing will be needed in a limited defense program for any of the other three purposes: to ensure
fair sharing, to get the goods where they are needed, or to
help make materials controls work? The answer is: probably
not to any great extent, because severe shortages are not
likely to be numerous. In the present defense effort, so far,
few if any acute shortages of consumer goods have appeared,
except temporarily.

Types of Rationing Schemes

When we do have to use rationing there are different
kinds to fit varying commodity or market characteristics.

1. Specific allotment of a single commodity on a showing of special need in accordance with specified criteria. This is usually called "certificate" rationing, because it is usually operated by giving a certificate to the person entitled to an allotment. This is a "one-at-a-time" allotment. Examples might be automobiles, tires, tractors, shoes and *extra* allotments of gasoline for special reasons.

2. Allotment of a certain quantity of an individual commodity in each period of time. This is often called "coupon" rationing because one method is to give to each consumer a book of coupons, which he may spend at designated rates per month or other period of time. Examples of coupon rationing might be coffee and sugar where each eligible individual is permitted to obtain with his coupons a certain quantity per month or per quarter.

3. Allotment of a whole family of items, many of which are substitutes for one another. This is sometimes called "point" rationing. Each item in the group is given a specified value in terms of points, which must be surrendered by the consumer in its purchase. Coupons in a ration book are then given specified point values. The rationing authorities can and do change the point values of the various items in accordance with shifts in relative supplies, or shifts in consumer preferences. That is, point values of items are set and changed so as to "clear the market" at all times. Point rationing lets each consumer spend his or her points as desired among several things—say, beef, lamb, fresh pork and ham.

Point rationing may be applied to all foods, to all clothing items, or to particular fields of each, such as meats, fats and oils; dairy products; canned fruits and vegetables; all men's clothing, work clothing excepted.

Rationing and Price Control

Sometimes it is maintained that rationing of a particular commodity or group of commodities would in itself prevent price increases and make ceiling price control unnecessary. There may be instances in which this would be true, especially if ration allotments were held somewhat below actual available supplies. In general, however, it does not appear that rationing can take the place of ceiling price control.

True, rationing can restrict the number of units of legal demand for a commodity to the number of units of available supply. But every holder of ration tickets may be willing to pay a fairly stiff price, if that is asked. This is quite likely to be so in the case of necessities for which there are no very satisfactory substitutes. Examples are automobiles, tires, gasoline, work gloves, eyeglasses, shoes and milk. In such cases, if sellers can administer their prices they will probably keep them above the levels that would be established by ceilings —that is, the levels set by an initial freeze modified by adjustments in accordance with policies and standards discussed above. Even where the number of sellers is so large that prices cannot be administered, the price for a commodity could settle above the level that a ceiling would maintain. However, in the case of a commodity of which the supply had been drastically curtailed, the competition of sellers trying to maintain something approaching normal volume might keep the price down to or below the level that would be established by a ceiling price.

To take another kind of example, rationing of meat could not in itself hold down prices of beef if producers of dairy and poultry products were free to bid high prices for the grain feeds used both by them and by those who feed cattle to "finish" them for market. Even if rationing were extended to become a closed system covering all consumer goods using grains, interproduct competition might bid up the materials cost.[14]

General Expenditure Rationing

General expenditure rationing would place a ceiling on the total spending of every consumer or household in a given period. Total demand thus would be made equal to total available supply of consumer goods and services at the desired price level. Consumers would be free to spread their spending as they liked over different items of food, clothing, and other goods and services. The scheme would be, in effect, a grand extension of "point rationing" to cover nearly everything.[15]

If it could be administered effectively, general expenditure rationing could be even more effective in curbing consumer demand than tax and credit measures. Like them, however, it could not in itself prevent wage rate increases and substantial increases in the prices of basic materials going into war or defense goods as well as consumer goods. Hence it is doubtful whether it would prevent inflation without direct price and wage controls.

Serious attention should be given to the problem of developing a workable scheme of general expenditure ration-

14. It may be added that a rationing scheme will not in itself prevent shifts in proportionate production from lower-priced to higher-priced items in a related group such as women's clothing.

15. We say "nearly" everything because administrative difficulties, or other considerations, might occasion omission of some things—perhaps entertainment—from the scheme.

ing for all-out war.[16] Such a scheme would be out of place in a defense program with the limited defense take that we are considering in this book.

16. An important beginning has been made in a recent book, *Mobilizing Resources for War*, by T. Scitovsky, E. S. Shaw and L. Tarshis, McGraw-Hill, New York, 1951. This report, prepared under the auspices of the Rand Corporation, gives special emphasis and attention to the very difficult and complex problems of designing an over-all scheme that makes sense in terms of economic principles. This is the first task. Thereafter, problems of detail, organization and administration, to say nothing of political elements, must be given hard and careful study before the workability of the scheme can be appraised.

10. Wage Controls

PRICE AND WAGE CONTROLS are equally important in a general program of direct stabilization controls. General price control cannot succeed without wage control, and vice versa. Loose wage control means that price ceilings must bend; loose control of living costs makes firm wage control impossible.

General government control of wages and salaries initially takes the form of a pay rate freeze. If control is to last more than a few months there must be provisions and standards for adjustments to correct inequities and to help deal with manpower shortages. When wage control is in effect during a limited defense program it may also be possible at times to make adjustments to give workers a part of the social and economic progress normal to the peacetime advance of a free society. The best administrative agency for general wage control seems to be a board composed of an equal number of representatives of labor, management and the public, as explained below. To do its job well, such a board must have jurisdiction over disputes. Selective wage control seems less practicable than selective price control.

Standards for wage adjustments are needed for a number of purposes of which the more important are: correction of substandard rates; keeping up with increases in living costs; reflection of increase in national productivity; determining interplant and intraplant differentials; handling manpower shortages.

Freeze and Adjustments

Under a wage and salary freeze, pay rates in effect at a

given time may not be increased except in accordance with approved standards for adjustment. The freeze and the provisions for adjustment must also cover all other terms of employment affecting the amount of pay, such as premiums for overtime, or for night or "graveyard" shifts.

Existing "fringe" benefits, for example, counting travel time in the hours worked, paid vacations, sick leave, pension plans and other health and welfare schemes should also be covered, since they affect costs even if they do not enter the workers' current income. There must be provisions and standards for adjustments in such benefits as well as in pay rates, if wage control stays in effect more than a few months.

If a union contract spells out explicitly the rates for the different types of labor and for overtime, the shift premiums and other terms of employment affecting workers' pay, and also the fringe benefits, it obviously is clear to labor and to management what has been frozen. Union contracts cover a large part of the economy. Written records of wage and salary rates and other benefits are available for another large part. Where there is no union contract or other written record, exactly what has been frozen may not be so clear—especially if both employer and employees favor a pay raise. However, because wage rates and terms of employment are so important to employers and employees, these groups are much more likely to know what is frozen than are sellers and buyers of commodities, especially ultimate consumers. In other words, the freeze technique is more effective in the case of wages and salaries than in the case of prices. Enforcement is also less of a problem, especially where there are union contracts that are, in effect, self-enforcing.

A pay rate freeze cuts across provisions in union contracts for automatic increases, unless these are given specific approval in the freeze regulation or in a subsequent order. This applies to the escalator clauses in union contracts calling for increases in basic wage rates to match increases in an index of consumer prices, or providing for periodic increases in rates to give workers a share of the benefits of increased productivity. A freeze also nullifies provisions for automatic increases in the general scale of fringe benefits, unless these are specifically authorized.[1]

A Tripartite Wage and Disputes Board

Experience seems to indicate that the best wage stabilization results usually will be obtained if administration is vested in a tripartite board with labor, management and the public equally represented. This gives labor and management full opportunity to present their points of view and their claims to one another and to the public members. The labor and management members bring to the job their technical knowledge of the complexities of labor-management relations and employment contracts. The public members can bring an impartial regard for the general interest and should work for the best attainable balance of interests between major groups. Tripartitism can also further compliance by workers and businessmen with the general spirit of the stabilization program and the specific rulings of the wage board. This is probably its greatest achievement.[2]

As a practical matter wage stabilization cannot be divorced

---

1. This does not, of course, mean that the freeze would interfere with a standard practice governing changes for individuals, such as increasing the number of days of paid vacations in accordance with length of employment with a company. It does mean that the *general scale* of days of paid vacation applicable to all employees could not be increased without approval.

2. Cf. W. E. Chalmers, M. Derber and W. H. McPherson, *Problems and Policies of Dispute Settlement and Wage Stabilization during World War II*, Bulletin No. 1009, Bureau of Labor Statistics, pp. 7 and 8.

from settlement of labor-management disputes. Many disputes are about wages or fringe benefits. In those concerned with other terms of employment there is often a tie-in with wages. For example, management or labor, or both, might consider the introduction of the union shop as the equivalent of so many cents per hour of wage increase. A separate disputes board would often have to get into wage questions, or hand many of the disputes over to the wage board or simply fail to settle them. Evidently both stabilization and dispute settlement should be in the hands of the same board.[3]

Beyond those just noted, there may be another advantage in this. The representation of labor and management on a board to handle dispute settlement as well as wage stabilization may constitute a kind of tacit no-strike, no-lockout pledge, at least on the part of the unions and the companies represented in the board membership (including regional boards) and of others who go along with the program. In wartime, labor and management usually are willing to enter a formal no-strike, no-lockout agreement. It is doubtful whether they will make a formal pledge in a defense period. Therefore the tacit agreement is important. The 1952 steel dispute and the ensuing strike was a dramatic instance of the breakdown of the "tacit pledge." It seems probable that such breakdowns will occur from time to time in the defense period when the compulsions of patriotism are less urgent than in full war.

Tripartitism in War and in Defense

In World War II, the War Labor Board was empowered to handle disputes along with wage stabilization, and the

3. *Ibid.,* p. 14.

joint administration of both responsibilities appeared to work very well.

In the present defense program, Executive Order 10233 (issued April 21, 1951) gave the Wage Stabilization Board limited jurisdiction in the settlement of disputes. The Board could not take jurisdiction on its own motion, but could deal with disputes in two circumstances: (1) when the parties to the dispute agreed to submit their differences to the Board for final decision, or for recommendations as to settlement; (2) when the President, believing the dispute substantially threatened the progress of national defense, referred the case to the Board for an investigation and a report to him with recommendations for equitable terms of settlement.

In June 1952, an amendment to the Defense Production Act removed from the Wage Stabilization Board most of the limited jurisdiction over disputes. Thereafter, all the Board could do in relation to disputes was to give advice, on request, to an affected party or to an interested federal agency as to the interpretation, or application to particular circumstances, of policies and regulations relating to stabilization of wages, salaries and other compensation.

Tripartitism really requires a large measure of self-regulation within whatever standards the law sets. Viewed in one way, it is a formal mechanism for helping business and labor exercise voluntary restraint. Representatives of business, labor and the public can work out stabilizing limits which are to be generally respected in wage determination.

In practice, the stabilization of wages by a tripartite board cannot be neat or entirely logical. In our democratic society, the results in this field, as in others, will reflect in part the pull and haul of organized groups. Experience in World War II indicates that in wartime wage stabilization can be both fair and on the whole workable. Experience in the defense period up to the end of 1952 has been inconclusive. Perhaps this is because no firm stabilization measures (except tax increases) were tried during the latter half of 1950, when inflationary pressures were severe. Hindsight suggests that if strong credit controls and a firm freeze of prices and wages had been put into effect soon after the Korean outbreak, these measures, together with the tax increases, could have convinced the public that the government meant business in preventing inflation—and no "maybes." This would have enabled the Wage Stabilization Board to take a much stronger line on holding wage rates.

Wage Control Cannot Be as Selective as Price Control

It is not practicable to have wage ceilings only in industries where the impact of the defense program creates shortages. Wage movements reflect political factors as well as economic pressures. When any one of the big, powerful unions obtains wage increases other unions will hasten to demand something similar—or better. Officers of a union that steadily falls behind others in wage advances will find it difficult to retain their posts. The attempt by other unions to equal or top the increases obtained in key wage bargains by unions in such industries as steel, automobiles, electrical equipment and rubber is a part of the price we pay for democracy in labor unions.

Thus, if wage control applies to any of the major unions it must apparently cover all, whether or not there is price control in industries where their members work. It must also cover unorganized labor where economic pressure would result in competitive wage bidding by employers.

This does not mean, however, that whenever there is

wage control it has to cover all workers. Exemptions can be made in fields where, in practice, unions cannot get wage increases soon enough or large enough to help start or accelerate a wage-price spiral, in fields where pay rates are only remotely related to the general wage and salary structure, and in government employment where wage increases usually lag well behind a general rise. Some examples of these different cases might be retail store clerks, employees of cleaning and dyeing establishments, hotel and restaurant employees, musicians, dancers, actors, baseball players and other entertainers, school teachers, policemen, firemen, and other public employees.[4]

Furthermore, wages of employees in most small establishments can be exempt from control without upsetting stabilization except, perhaps, in full mobilization. However, to this general principle there are some exceptions. For example, in a defense build-up there will be for a time an acute shortage of tool and die designers and makers. Many of these work in small establishments and many others for auto companies or other large manufacturers. Wage control in cases like this must obviously go across the board.

With inflationary pressure in most of the economy, general wage control is in order, with such exceptions as those noted above. In the early part of a defense build-up, or after a hump is passed, there may be times in which strong inflationary pressure is limited to industries producing defense goods, materials important in defense production, and, perhaps, some consumer goods the output of which has been cur-

4. Wages of government employees can obviously be controlled by legislative and administrative action. Legislatures do not usually raise wages of public employees ahead of other wages! In a manpower shortage individual government agencies may, however, go in for labor pirating by upgrading and other devices unless restrained through administrative control by civil service commissions, a wage stabilization agency, or other authorities.

tailed owing to defense demands for materials. If most of the rest of the economy is buoyant—that is, generally prosperous without inflationary pressure—there will be danger of a spiral starting in the defense area where inflationary pressure is strong and then spreading through the rest of the economy.

The Problem of Selective Control

This situation calls for selective government price control —ceilings on materials and products under inflationary pressure and close pricing and renegotiation by procurement authorities. If selective government wage control were feasible, that would also be in order. Its impracticability presents a dilemma. Can the spiral be prevented by a combination of selective government price control and voluntary wage control with or without government guidance? Or will general wage control be necessary, and will this have to be accompanied by general price control to gain acceptance by labor? Only experience can answer these questions. We should make every effort to improve our capacity to get through such periods without general wage and price controls, and without inflation.

If voluntary wage control is the reliance, management and labor must have some public guidance. Voluntary control may not be effective in any case. We can be sure that it will not amount to much if labor and management are requested merely to avoid "inflationary" wage increases. There must be guiding rules of the game in the form of stabilization limits, or, to put it another way, standards for permissible wage increases. The guiding rules should probably be worked out by a tripartite commission composed of leaders of labor, management and the general public, in order to command as much respect as possible. And if this device should work well in the defense period it might become a part of our regular equipment to deal with the inflation problem in ordinary peacetime, if and when that returns.

There is always a danger that disputes in industries essential to defense will be settled by inflationary wage increases —increases that go far beyond the rules of the stabilization game. This is true with government as well as voluntary wage control. In both cases the problem of designing fair wage standards which also will help needed manpower redistribution without inflation is much less difficult than the problem of getting major labor and management groups to accept responsibility for stabilization. This problem lies in a field where the author of this report has no special competence to suggest solutions.

In Chapter 9, we saw that types of price ceilings and coverage of price control, as well as pricing standards, afford scope for change from a fuller to a more limited direct controls program, or vice versa. In the case of wage controls, most of the change has to occur in wage standards, since it is not possible to alter greatly either the type of ceiling or the coverage of wage control.

Standards for Wage Adjustment

Once wage rates or other factors affecting pay and benefits are frozen, the principal job of the wage authorities is to devise and administer standards for adjustments to remove inequities and to help deal with manpower shortages. Given these objectives most of the adjustments will be upward. However, reductions in some particular rates may be a part of a general overhauling of rate differentials for the various jobs in a plant.

In full war mobilization, standards for wage adjustment,

like standards for price adjustment, must be very tight. And during the defense period wage standards, like pricing standards, will need to be tight whenever inflationary pressure is severe. If wage controls are needed after inflationary pressure abates somewhat they can be looser, again like pricing standards, and they should be, in order to permit labor to participate in general economic and social advance. Furthermore, maintenance of tight standards for several years might retard the growth of certain industries or regions and interfere with other desirable, dynamic developments in the economy.

The following sections sketch tight and less restrictive standards for each type of wage rate adjustment for which such a difference seems possible.

Correction of Substandard Rates

The removal of substandard wage rates has become a widely accepted principle. A wage freeze should not interfere with this. The wage board may deem it wise to use a somewhat higher figure for minimum standard rates than that currently embodied in law, either to take account of some inflation of living costs not yet reflected in the law, or because it is felt that the defense effort and the general health of the economy will be advanced by partly reducing the differentials between the lowest-paid and the better-paid jobs.

In adjustments to remove substandard rates, a difference between tight and loose standards seems pointless unless a looser standard (that is, a standard permitting a larger adjustment) seems desirable during strong inflationary pressure. For it is at such times that the reasons for advancing the minimum rates are most likely to prevail.

Adjustments to Keep Up With Living Costs

In peacetime, there is a general tendency for most wage and salary rates to increase sooner or later when there has been a marked increase in the level of prices, say 10 per cent or more. If we have a substantial inflation of prices, proportionate increases of wage and salary rates (and also profit rates and other income rates) are desirable on the grounds both of fairness and of efficient operation of the economy. Much of the harm from inflation comes, as we saw in Chapter 2, from its uneven impact, with many prices and many wage and other income rates lagging far behind the average rise.

Considerations of equity, morale and efficiency call for provision in a stabilization program for adjustments in basic wage, salary and other income rates to match substantial increases in living costs sooner or later—that is, if living costs are allowed to rise. This is true even in full war, to say nothing of a defense program. Assurance that the relative position of workers in the economy will not be lowered by emergency wage control is probably necessary, along with the same assurance to other groups, to make possible a balance of interests without which neither successful stabilization nor a maximum war or defense effort is possible.

Some argue in favor of letting the price level rise while holding down wage, salary and other personal income rates as a means of bringing about a necessary cut in per capita consumption to make way for war or defense production. But it would be difficult—probably impossible—to devise practicable measures of control of prices and personal income rates that would result in equitable sharing in such a cut in consumption. Raising taxes is a surer and fairer method.

To lower consumption by tax increases means that Congress can write the ticket much more precisely than it ever can with price and wage controls where administrative discretion must have broad scope. A tax bill also affords an over-all view of the problem of equitable sharing of sacrifice and the opportunity to set out the basic pattern in one legislative measure. Imposing the sacrifice principally by tax increases also makes it possible to keep a pattern of prices, wage and salary rates, and other income rates—before taxes—which indicates to the various groups that emergency stabilization controls are not being used to impair their prewar or predefense positions in the economy. Of course, in full war, when it is probably impossible to balance the budget without harm to the war effort, some kind of forced saving will be needed in addition to higher taxes. This will have to be worked into the general pattern for fair sharing of necessary cuts in consumption.

The tie between wage and salary rates and living costs here advocated is in fact a kind of guarantee that emergency wage control will not be allowed to injure the relative positions of groups of workers for the "more normal" future when controls are off. But such an assurance does not require either automatic or frequent adjustment of rates, and such adjustments should not be made automatically or frequently in times of strong inflationary pressure, either in the defense period or in wartime.

Treatment of the Escalators

In Chapter 8, we saw that a principal element in the general strategy of stabilization is to suspend all automatic escalators in periods of severe inflationary pressure. At such times, price levels cannot be held absolutely flat in each year, to say nothing of each quarter. To permit frequent or automatic cost-of-living wage adjustments under these conditions would be to promote the spiral of price and wage increases. Hence at these times such escalator clauses in all wage contracts should be suspended. In such periods, also, the wage control authorities should not apply any general cost-of-living wage adjustment formula, until after the consumers' price index (or other appropriate measure) has risen substantially—say, perhaps, more than 6 per cent in a twelve-month period or more than 10 per cent in twenty-four months. When, as and if such a tripping point is reached and the cost-of-living wage adjustment provision goes into effect, then cost-of-living escalator clauses should be allowed to operate in conformity with the general provision.

Use of a Catch-Up Formula

If a considerable increase in consumer prices occurred before a general wage freeze, and some wage rates had risen less than consumer prices, a "catch-up" formula for wage rate adjustments would be desirable, both as part of the general guarantee discussed above and as a means of handling inequities among groups whose wage rates had not moved together. In World War II, the Little Steel formula was adopted by the War Labor Board in July 1942, as a "catch-up" formula. It permitted an increase in straight-time hourly earnings of 15 per cent above January 1941 levels. In the present defense program, the Wage Stabilization Board adopted a similar policy after the general freeze of wage rates in January 1951. This policy permitted all wage rates to go up 10 per cent above the levels in effect on January 15, 1950.

With a general wage freeze in effect during a period of severe inflationary pressure, no cost-of-living rate adjustments should be made other than the "catch-up" adjustments—unless there is a substantial rise in living costs, as discussed above.

When there is a decline in inflationary pressure, permitting a shift to more limited direct stabilization control, the wage regulations can allow full compensation for living cost increases occurring after the freeze went into effect. This means lifting the suspension of escalator clauses and of provisions for reopening the wage sections of a contract while the rest is still in effect. It also means permitting wage adjustments to keep abreast of consumer price increases at intervals agreed on by labor and management or, where there is no union, whenever management wishes to make such compensation. The wage standard here discussed puts a loose rein on general wage advances while permitting increases corresponding to the normal movements in a peacetime economy. Thus it is akin to the percentage-profit-margin industry earnings standard, which has similar effects in the field of price.

A policy of permitting full compensation for increases in the average of consumer prices was adopted by the Wage Stabilization Board in 1951. General wage rate adjustments were permitted (on top of the 10 per cent "catch-up" adjustments) equal to the increase in the consumers' price index above its level on January 15, 1951.

Adjustments to Reflect Increase in Productivity

In ordinary peacetime there is a general tendency for wage rates to move upward over the years with increasing man-hour productivity for the country as a whole. A periodic rise in wage rates is one way in which labor shares in the increased output. Ordinarily, however, these rises should not go beyond the average increase in productivity for the whole economy. Larger increases, if numerous, would be a strong inflationary factor, simultaneously pushing up costs and demand.

During severe inflationary pressure no wage adjustments for reason of increasing productivity should be permitted. The job is to counter a serious buying surge or wage-price spiral, or both, and wage adjustments must be limited to the few necessary to remove serious inequities or to help, together with other measures, deal with acute manpower shortages in defense production. Wage adjustments to afford a share in rising productivity are not in this class. Moreover, at times of severe inflationary pressure in the defense period, all increased productivity in the economy probably will need to go into expansion of defense production. This leaves no room for wage increases to permit workers to raise consumption in step with expanding national output. The same is true, of course, for farmers, dividend receivers, professional men and women and the other self-employed.

At times when inflationary pressure is moderate and all or most of the annual increase in productivity of the economy can go into civilian consumption, productivity adjustments should be permitted everywhere so long as they do not exceed the average increase in productivity for the economy as a whole. More generous advances for labor in some industries, to reflect advances in productivity beyond the average, would set up unworkable differentials among workers of the same type and skill in different industries. Given the political forces at work in the unions this would prove inflationary, for unions in the industries with lower productivity gains would base their wage demands on the increases secured by unions in industries with higher productivity advances. What they got might exceed the average productivity increase in the economy, even though it fell short of the biggest wage increases.

The 1950 contract between the General Motors Corporation and the United Automobile Workers, which bases annual productivity adjustments on a figure approximating the past average increase for the economy as a whole, represents good policy for peacetime and for defense years when per capita civilian consumption can be allowed to increase. Our system stands for a steady rise in the standard of living. The promise of this is a stimulus to bring it about—a stimulus we want to keep.

In the present defense program, the Wage Stabilization Board permitted productivity adjustments, as well as cost-of-living adjustments. Whether inflationary pressure was severe enough after WSB came into operation to make this unwise is a hard question.

It is often suggested that at times of heavy inflationary pressure cost-of-living and productivity adjustments should be continued but paid in bonds redeemable only after the inflationary emergency was over. Conceivably, this would be a sensible policy under some circumstances in the defense period, but reflection suggests that this should not be the rule. In an inflationary emergency lasting not more than one, two or three years, complete elimination of these adjustments would be wise and should prove practicable. If the emergency should last more than five years, there would be great uncertainty as to when it was going to end and whether spending the accumulation of bonds would not itself kindle a severe inflation.

Interplant Adjustments

Interplant adjustments deal with differences in rates for

the same or similar work in different plants within a labor market area. They may concern differences between plants in the same industry or in different industries. Interplant adjustments involve both inequities and manpower problems. A general freeze continues whatever wage inequities exist at the time it goes into effect. It also freezes some rate relations between plants that were so far out of line as to exert a one-way pull on labor. A plant "caught with its wages down" may have been ready to raise them when its contract expired; perhaps a new contract with higher rates had already been negotiated, but was not yet in force.

Tight standards for interplant adjustments may take either or both of two forms. The first is a narrow definition of the standard of comparison—that is, the group of workers in the area considered to be doing the same or most nearly similar work. The second is the selection of the rate among the various rates in that group of workers to which lower rates may be adjusted. The standard used by the War Labor Board in World War II, the "minimum sound and tested going rate" in the area, is a tight standard. This was usually defined as the lowest cluster of rates in the whole array of rates for that kind of labor in the area. Where there was no cluster below the average, the standard was defined as 10 per cent below the average.

A less restrictive standard would be a broader definition of the standard of comparison and permission to adjust up to the average rate in the area.

Intraplant Adjustments

Workers' efficiency is ordinarily promoted by sound schemes for promotion and merit increases, by frequent re-evaluation of jobs and reclassification, and the like. In a tight manpower situation, however, these can degenerate into plain upgrading to get around the rules of wage and salary stabilization. When the less restrictive standards for wages are adequate this presents no problem.

When tight wage standards are in order, upgrading and similar practices constitute an exceedingly difficult problem. Unless stabilizing limits are set for such increases the door will be open to extensive evasion of other wage regulations. Experience in World War II suggests that an effective way to deal with this problem is to set limits both for the increases allowed individual employees and for the total sum allowed a plant for such increases in a given period.[5] Restrictions would also be needed on hiring new employees at rates above the minimum rate in the range for each job.

Adjustments to Ease Manpower Shortages

In Chapter 8, we noted that the number of wage increases designed to attract manpower into particular jobs or locations should be limited whenever inflationary pressure is strong enough to require general wage and price control. Otherwise the incentive wage increases would be both self-defeating and inflationary. Some increases for this purpose will be unavoidable. It is difficult to define in advance standards for such adjustments. These must be worked out case by case, under the general principle (strictly observed) that the adjustment should never exceed the smallest needed, together with the use of all other practicable measures, to overcome the particular shortage.

At times of milder inflationary pressure, standards for this sort of wage adjustment can be less restrictive, but limits are

5. General Regulation 5 of the Wage Stabilization Board sets restrictions of this sort.

still needed. Even in ordinary peacetime prosperity there is a danger that wage increases may outrun the average increase in productivity, resulting in a "push-up" inflation. The added impetus of defense wage increases would heighten this danger.

Fringe Benefits

Paid vacations, pension plans, health and welfare schemes and the like are generally considered a part of our social and economic progress, and an important advantage in our economic struggle with communism. When the inflation danger is only moderate there should probably be no restriction on the introduction of new kinds of fringe benefits or on the spread of existing types.

When inflationary pressure is severe, some restrictions are in order. As a rule, the payments involved in fringe benefits do not go directly into workers' pockets but they add directly to current production costs. At such times it is reasonable to prohibit, for the time being, the introduction of new types of fringe benefits. However, as in the case of wage rates, some "catch-up" standard is desirable. This can take the form of permitting adoption in an industry, or a labor market area, of fringe benefits already the prevailing practice there. This seems to be the policy followed by the Wage Stabilization Board in the present defense program, except for health and welfare schemes where the Board has set specific standards and permits everyone to come up to these whether or not they are already the prevailing practice. Given the paramount importance of improving the general level of health and welfare—from the standpoint of military security and as an example of what a free society can do— this distinction between health and welfare benefits and others seems wise in the defense period, even when there is strong inflationary pressure.

Wage Control Essential to Stabilization

Government wage control is a difficult business at best. Possibly it cannot be made effective without the compulsions of full war. Another possibility is that, although it seems to be working well, the resulting wage increases may prove to be greater than those that would be set by collective bargaining, without government participation.

Voluntary wage control is also a difficult business. The record so far indicates that it can accomplish something, but there is still a large question as to how much. If we really fear inflation as much as sensible Americans should, we ought to do everything possible to make both government wage control and voluntary wage control effective when there is need for one or both in the defense period. This means also, of course, that we should do all we can to make price control work, whenever it is needed, and that we should be sure to use unfaltering fiscal and credit controls all the time. These are the "iron men" of stabilization, but there are times when direct controls are indispensable.

11. Basic Problems and Policies

By J. M. CLARK[1]

THE SUBJECT of the present volume—"direct controls" —consists of policies acting directly on supply, or on the mobilization of resources for supply, and on the prices charged for products and for specific means of production, including wages of labor and rents. The most controversial items are compulsory controls of prices and wages; but equally essential, as parts of a rounded program of direct controls, are priorities and allocations of scarce materials, plus inventory controls and orders limiting particular products or requiring conservation in the use of scarce materials— scarce, that is, in relation to existing "effective demand." Rationing of a number of scarce and essential consumer goods is needed in all-out war, but apparently not in the kind of defense emergency now in prospect.

What Professor Wallace has undertaken in this volume is to present the requirements of a program that would be

1. In the present volume, the usual policy report by the Committee is replaced by this personal statement, for which the writer alone is responsible, and to which the other members of the Committee were invited to add dissenting footnotes. Professor Wallace, as author of the volume, felt that he should take no part in Committee comments, and Professor Schultz' views were such as to make it seem unprofitable to ask him to join in a Committee statement on the highly controversial subject of direct controls. I have profited by comments from all members of the Committee; and in this I fear I have increased Professor Schultz' burdens, perhaps unfairly. Instead of letting my statement stand, with all the imperfections revealed by his first proposed footnotes, I have revised it, incorporating my version of points of his with which I was already in agreement, and fortifying my argument at points where differences appeared to remain. I rationalized this as an attempt to make definite the nature of our remaining differences, aside from shortcomings of formulation. But to meet this challenge, he might have to write another volume, with a different approach and emphasis, to which single footnotes on particular statements could not possibly do justice.—J. M. CLARK

adequate for meeting the strains of a defense emergency. He has not undertaken an analysis and appraisal of the recent programs of direct controls. That would call for an extensive study of a different kind, and an evaluation beyond the resources of the present Twentieth Century Fund Committee.

However, this study recognizes that direct controls do not exist in an insulated vacuum. It accords recognition, though not primary attention, to numerous policies which act directly, but by other methods than compulsory orders. Voluntary methods are especially needed in the mobilization of manpower. In addition, and likely to be neglected because they are always with us (on the principle of the invisibility of the postman), there is the large and important field of procurement policies for commodities. This includes not only pricing policies, but the placing of orders and selection of suppliers, and policy as to "taking work to the workers"; also as to the degree of specialization of plants which should be followed in carrying out the basic policy of adding defense capacity to civilian-goods capacity rather than converting civilian capacity to defense use. These can have considerable effect on the capacity of the economy to handle future fluctuations in the defense program with a minimum of disturbance.

Functions and Limitations of Indirect Controls

A major premise of any such study, for an economy of the American sort, is that indirect controls are to be preferred to direct controls, for all functions they are capable of performing. Furthermore, the extent of the need for direct controls, the strains put upon them, and the possibility of success in meeting these strains are conditioned by the character and adequacy of the indirect controls actually employed —whether or not they do all they are capable of doing. In view of this interrelationship, Professor Wallace has based his study on the assumption that the indirect controls do their part, without which the direct controls could not hope to succeed in doing the part appropriate to them. This assumption cannot be reduced to a precise and noncontroversial blueprint for the indirect controls, as the companion volumes in this series bear witness. But the intent of this volume is to avoid describing, or impliedly advocating, a stretching of direct controls beyond their proper function, to make up for deficiencies in indirect controls.

The main purpose of the indirect controls is to limit total spendable income and credit funds to approximately the amount that can buy the expected physical product at noninflationary prices, this limitation being accomplished via fiscal, monetary and credit measures. These measures can have some selective effect as between different commodities or branches of production, but this is supplementary to their principal effect on total volume of spending. "Noninflationary prices" cannot, for this purpose, be identified with a rigidly unchanging price index. It is expected and desired that physical production should expand, and should be directed to the most essential uses. This is favored if some prices rise, and also some wage rates (though in most cases moderate increases are sufficient for the purpose in hand, and immoderate increases may be self-defeating). And the desired expansion would not be favored if every rise of a particular price had to be offset by a decline of some other price.

Attempts to bring about such declines by indirect controls would be likely to fail, or to result in contracting production.

"Inflation" implies a condition in which rises have become general and, generally, progressively self-reinforcing. The goal of indirect controls adequate to prevent inflationary excess demand, in this somewhat elastic sense, is economically attainable for the *general average* of conditions in the kind of defense emergency which is now in prospect, if the calamity of all-out war can be averted.

Full-Scale War Requires Direct Controls

It is generally recognized that if all-out war should supervene, controls in all the general categories, direct and indirect, would need to be applied with the utmost promptness and vigor. With all their unavoidable costs and crudities, direct controls would be accepted by the country as lesser evils than those which would result if all-out war mobilization were left to be handled by the struggles of a "free market," limited only by what indirect controls could do. No feasible tax system, even with "voluntary" savings added, could possibly divert to public use as large a percentage of the country's dollar income as the percentage of its real resources which all-out war would call for. And the total volume of credit would need to be large enough for ample expansion. Then if nonessential production were free to bid for funds in a free market against essential production, the result would inevitably be a considerable diversion of resources to nonessential uses (including needlessly swollen inventories, amounting to hoarding) with corresponding loss of essential production and delay of mobilization under conditions in which delay could be fatal, and also a violent and unproductive bidding-up of prices and money wages. With this goes a grossly inequitable distribution of scarce consumer products, and the broader income inequities of a violent price-wage inflation. This appears inevitable in the absence of direct controls, unless fiscal and credit controls became so rigorously selective as to amount to direct controls, carrying the selective feature far beyond the supplementary role which this committee has elsewhere assigned to it.[2] It is in face of these conditions that modern nations, faced with modern all-out war, have uniformly elected to include a wide assortment of direct controls in their arsenals of economic weapons.[3]

The country can endure the direct controls in an emergency that is expected to come to a definite end in a moderate time, after which the controls are expected to be removed. And experience indicates that, with the help of wartime morale, the controls can work well enough to accomplish a substantial mitigation of the evils against which they are directed.

2. See Committee Report in A. G. Hart, *Defense and the Dollar,* Twentieth Century Fund, New York, 1953, p. 195, No. 2 under "Specific Recommendations."

3. I dissent from the foregoing paragraph for several reasons. It states that no feasible combination of fiscal and monetary controls can avert a "violent price-wage inflation," accompanied by hampering of mobilization, in the event of all-out war. This I do not believe to be true. I should advocate holding the supply of money in check, and letting changes in relative prices carry as much of the organizational load as possible, and much more than the above paragraph implies. Some rise in the general price level may even be desirable under all-out war conditions. But that the money supply must become so much larger that all or most of the functions of relative prices will have to be taken over by other controls—this, in my judgment, need not occur.

There is also the implication that no matter what the particular wartime conditions may be, direct controls will be the "lesser evils." This is certainly too sweeping. Under particular wartime conditions, there may be an exceedingly strong case for the rationing of some consumer goods which are thought of as most "necessary." This means mainly food. But even in the case of food, the particular conditions may be such that it will be possible to postpone rationing of food, for example, if an all-out war were to put great strain on international shipping and transport and as a consequence the United States, at least for a time, were to find it difficult to transport as much food to other countries as formerly. This is one set of particular conditions which might postpone the rationing of food in the United States in the event of an all-out war.—T. W. SCHULTZ

In a defense emergency of indefinite prospective duration, and without the support of wartime morale, the dangers of continued and general use of direct controls are much greater, for reasons amply indicated in this volume and in the earlier volume, *Defense without Inflation.* All-out war can go a long way in pushing normal peacetime activities to one side; the defense drive must learn to live with them, and they with it; and continuous general use of direct controls would place the health of the peacetime economic functions in jeopardy, even if the controls were effective, while the likelihood of breakdown would be greatly increased. To the utmost extent possible, indirect controls should bear the load.

If inflation occurs in such a defense emergency because of inadequate indirect controls, the indicated recommendation for policy is clear: "make the indirect controls adequate." If inflation persists, in harmful degree, because of persistent failure to follow this course, the problem becomes more perplexing, involving a choice of evils. The country must either endure a harmful degree of inflation or overwork the direct controls, with the risk that they will be broken down and discredited when some greater emergency arrives for which direct controls are more urgently needed.

Why Direct Controls Are Needed

But, to return to the case envisaged in this volume, of a defense drive with adequate indirect controls. There remain three forms of inflationary pressure, arising in certain phases of the drive, which the indirect controls would not be able to handle, or not completely, and which call for the use of direct controls. And the present volume examines the ways in which direct controls, if handled with discriminating skill and vigor, can supply what is missing, without either lapsing into ineffectual desuetude or hardening into a permanent straitjacket for the economy. These three forms of pressure are the following.

1. Waves of speculative or scare buying, responding to unforeseeable changes in the situation and financed to a considerable extent in ways that would escape the more obvious forms of credit control.

It is characteristic of such waves that they can turn a fairly normal supply situation into one of artificially induced scarcity, through the struggle of buyers to build up more-than-normal inventories. Less spectacular pressures would result from the impossibility of adjusting the indirect controls promptly and accurately enough to keep pace with fluctuations in the volume of the defense effort. If the price impact of these waves of stress were unchecked, it could spread and be perpetuated by the "ratchet action" resulting from resistance to downward movement of prices and wages, which is coming to be recognized as a feature of our present economy. Well-devised direct controls could check this price impact. Available methods include allocation of essential materials, checks on inventory hoarding, and perhaps a temporary price freeze—presumably imposed after some increases had taken place. Indirect controls could—and this would be highly important—limit the pressures the direct controls would have to deal with to such as they could handle, and make the need for general direct controls temporary.[4]

4. Surely speculative buying can serve a useful function; surely some firms should acquire more credit to expand output of war goods and therefore should "escape the more obvious forms of credit control," while other firms contract operations and their use of credit; and surely some product and factor prices should rise rapidly and far relative to other prices.—T. W. SCHULTZ

Expansion of operations is one thing, and inventory hoarding another. Hoarding may be done both by firms that are expanding operations and by

2. Special scarcities of particular items, largely essential materials and intermediate products.

In most cases, output can be increased, but only after an interval longer than the duration of the fluctuations just spoken of. Such scarcities are, of course, relative to total demand, including defense and private demands. Experience indicates private demand will either not decrease, or not nearly as much as defense demand increases, if it is limited only by indirect controls, acting mainly on the total volume of spending power, and selective to only a limited extent. Then if, in resulting periods of stress, defense must secure its supplies by outbidding private demand in a free market, the urgency of defense demand is likely to result in bidding prices up beyond what serves any purpose in increasing supply. And, especially if buyers are free to hoard inventories, there is still a likelihood that defense needs will not be fully met. Such a situation gives ground for controls which are likely to progress rapidly from priorities to allocations and to production programming, and to be accompanied by selective price ceilings which would last longer than the peaks of general inflationary pressure should last, if indirect controls were adequate.

3. The familiar price-wage-price spiral.

This can start at any one of numerous points in the economy, from which it can spread and cumulate. It does not depend on the existence of a general inflationary excess of demand, though it is facilitated by excess demand at

---

those that are contracting. Firms working on war orders do not need to "escape" credit controls, in the sense I had in mind—banks will grant them loans. The point is that firms can find ways to finance inventory hoarding even if regular bank credit is tight. "Rapidly and far" is a matter of degree. My view is that in most cases a moderate increase is sufficient for all useful stimulative effects.—J. M. CLARK

particular points, by the public urgency behind the defense demand, and by a general state of strong demand, close to, but not necessarily up to, the "full employment" level. The key point here is the difficulty or impossibility of checking a wage-price spiral merely by limiting total buying power through indirect controls. Eliminating an inflationary excess of demand would not be sufficient; restriction would have to go far enough to create deliberately induced unemployment—which is hardly thinkable in such a setting. The wage-price spiral may persist in milder form independently of a defense drive, as may also the principle of "ratchet action," introducing a moderate inflationary bias into the peacetime economy.[5]

These three elements, in the absence of allocations, and of direct controls of prices and wages, and despite the presence of "adequate" indirect controls, would be likely to introduce inflationary pressures. The first, speculative waves, would be general and short, coming at unpredictable intervals. The second, particular scarcities, would be longer lasting but still temporary, occurring in the period of building up productive capacity, and would be localized, but with ramifying effects. The third, the wage-price spiral, is more chronic. At present (December 1952) this seems to be the chief source of possible inflationary pressure in the near future, the other sources being inactive or quite limited. They could be revived by developments increasing defense tension, or a recession could occur as the defense program passes its hump.

Seriousness of Continued Moderate Inflation

As to whether these three kinds of inflationary pressure,

---

5. The preceding three paragraphs underrate greatly the role and capacity of fiscal and monetary controls of the indirect class.—T. W. SCHULTZ

when they are active, warrant the use of direct controls, judgment hinges largely on how seriously one regards a given amount of inflation. Professor Wallace has done a service by indicating that even 3 per cent a year, if continued for fifteen or twenty years, becomes a very serious matter. The present writer would be inclined to name a lower limit —say from 2 per cent to $2\frac{1}{2}$ per cent—beyond which substantial harm begins, if this average rate of increase is indefinitely continued. In the two and a half years since the outbreak of hostilities in Korea, this country has gone through about eight months during which consumer prices rose $8\frac{1}{2}$ per cent (or at an annual rate of $12\frac{3}{4}$ per cent), followed by a longer period marked by a rise at an average annual rate of about $2\frac{1}{2}$ per cent. The latter period has been spoken of as one of "uneasy equilibrium," in which it appears that general inflationary demand has subsided (though it may not have wholly disappeared), while the elements of a wage-price spiral are still present. But it is notable that this "equilibrium" has shown an upward-creeping bias, uncomfortably close to the limit suggested by Professor Wallace, and slightly above the lower limit envisaged by the present writer, if the trend is indefinitely continued. Will it so continue?

As to this, informed opinions differ. Prices of raw foodstuffs may fall, though this may be outweighed by a slow rise of other prices, under the push of wage increases exceeding the average rise in physical productivity. This could build up a troublesome discrepancy between the course of agricultural and other prices. One possibility is a mild recession—say in 1954 or 1955—in which case the emphasis of policy would shift to antirecession measures. If the recession were kept mild, it might not wholly eliminate the wage-price spiral, or the relative disadvantage of agriculture. Or something like the recent rate of upward creep might continue, and might be interspersed with intervals of stronger inflationary pressure, tending to a more rapid rise. This is one of the possibilities which the economy should be prepared to meet, if it occurs.

It is to be earnestly hoped that indirect controls would be sufficient, during most of the defense drive, to check further pressures toward price inflation, if and when they arise, or at least hold them to a relatively harmless rate of increase. For this purpose, they would need to be tighter, during inflationary intervals, than those we have had hitherto. And in view of the factors treated in this volume, indirect controls alone cannot guarantee complete protection against inflationary movements, in all parts of the economy or at all times during a defense drive, especially those due to a wage-price spiral.

Dilemmas of Limited and Temporary Direct Controls

Informed opinions differ also as to whether current direct controls have any substantial restraining effect. Out of this grow the further questions: "If wage controls are abandoned, and price controls are limited to such special scarcities as may continue, will serious inflation result now or later; and if this threat exists, could it be kept within safe bounds by continuing direct controls that would be general, but flexible, varying with varying conditions?"

Such a system of flexible controls, while logical, encounters a number of practical dilemmas arising from the interrelations of wage and price controls, compounded with the differences in timing of the three forms of inflationary pressure for which indirect controls are insufficient. So far as the direct pull of excess demand is concerned, general price controls could be temporary if indirect controls were adequate; and selective controls of special scarcities could be tolerated for longer periods without serious results. But the problem is complicated by the fact that wage controls appear to need to be general if they are to be effective, and that effective wage control appears to be contingent on general price control. It follows that if the wage-price spiral is a continuing factor, to an extent requiring wage controls if it is to be checked, suspension of general price controls carries the penalty of releasing the wage-price spiral and submitting to whatever creeping inflation it may produce. This could be a difficult choice of evils.

But if general price controls are retained to deal with this continuing factor, then a "tight" system, suited to a limited period of strong excess demand, would need to be converted into one loose enough to be continued for a considerable time without too seriously impairing normal business incentives and flexibilities. This raises the question as to whether such a loose system of controls could be effective enough in controlling prices to be worth its cost and accompanying disadvantages; and the further administrative problem as to whether the same personnel would be capable of switching back and forth between tight and loose standards of control —a dilemma for which the present volume suggests something like a "two-platoon system" as a possible answer. It appears enormously important that this dilemma should be avoided or minimized: that is, that the total price situation, including any element of wage-price spiral that may persist, should not add up to a harmful degree of inflation.

State of Readiness Needed

In the light of the possibility of either full-scale war or renewed waves of strong inflationary pressure, it appears that, even if general price controls are abandoned or suspended, a state of readiness for prompt resumption needs to be maintained. This raises problems as to what legislative authorizations should be kept in force, and whether skeleton forces or an observation-post organization should be continued. If harmful inflation were resumed, after the disbanding of active control staffs, there would be a problem as to whether a skeleton organization, kept in being, could succeed in "holding the line" temporarily with a general price-freeze order, which could be put in effect more promptly than fiscal measures, and with more positive effect on prices than either fiscal or credit measures could be sure of having, in the face of sudden inflationary pressure.

If it were not a case of full-scale war, and if the price freeze were promptly followed up by adequate fiscal and credit measures, these indirect controls might conceivably afford sufficient restraints on inflation. In that case, the freeze order could be rescinded before it became necessary—as it soon would—to replace it with ceilings of the formula or dollars-and-cents types. But this easy outcome could not be counted on, and the interval would need to be used to recruit an active controlling force as rapidly as possible. Such a policy of demobilizing controls, and relying on the power of a freeze order to tide over any future renewed emergency, would be a gamble, but one that appears worth taking at any time when the relaxation of inflationary pressures permits suspension of general price controls. Success depends on indirect controls that are not only strong but promptly adaptable to changing conditions

All these problems and dilemmas appear in Professor Wallace's report; and, in the nature of the case, beset as it is with uncertainties, no sure and simple solution can be offered. Policy must proceed on a basis of calculated risks, in the light of a weighing of what appear to be the most serious dangers.

The weakest link in the chain would seem to be the control of wages, which cannot succeed without voluntary compliance. Indeed, anything else would be inconsistent with this country's basic freedoms, combined as they are with the sanctioning of national labor organization and its present equipment of powerful tactics. The noninflationary standard for wage increases would limit them approximately to the rate of increase in average real net product per worker in the economy as a whole, from which the workers' share of defense requirements must be subtracted, in the form of taxes or otherwise. Even this presupposes that the initial wage is noninflationary. Any excess must represent gains for labor at the expense of the relative shares of other factors; and the room for such gains is so limited as to be unimportant, in comparison with the long-run increase in product, and the diversions necessitated by defense. Major gains by particular groups are made only partly at the expense of holders of fixed-income securities, and in greater degree at the expense of other workers, creating a tendency for these other groups to make good at least part of what they have lost, absolutely or relatively.

The gains which strongly organized labor groups have come to expect and demand go far beyond this noninflationary standard; and a labor leader places his position in some danger if he does not deliver something like what is expected, or what other unions are getting. For the resulting dilemma there is no obvious and simple answer, because there is no simple formula for substituting statesmanship for politics, either in government, in intraunion organization or in those features of business policy which call for economic statesmanship rather than for narrowly "business-like" motivation. The necessary conditions for full success in this matter will not be met tomorrow, nor the day after.

In Conclusion

In conclusion, it appears that the greatest single danger, and one that has been repeatedly stressed in this chapter, is that, at times of inflationary pressure of the various sorts here considered, insufficient indirect controls will place on the direct controls a burden they cannot successfully carry, and will result in their being continued when they should be relaxed or suspended. The dangers of such continuance need not be reiterated.

At the risk of being banal, one may say that if everyone accepts a share of the burdens of defense, the total load will be less than if everyone tries his utmost to escape, and to shift the burdens to others. In an economy that behaves in the former fashion, there is a substantial and useful place for direct controls, in filling the gaps which are analyzed in this volume, and doing the things the indirect controls cannot do. But direct controls cannot successfully be asked to make up for the shortcomings of all the groups in the economy, and of all other types of controls.

Index